Dr. Danger Forward

*Dedicated to the members of Company B, 1st Med. Bn.,
who served during World War II*

Doctor Danger Forward

A World War II Memoir of a Combat Medical Aidman, First Infantry Division

by
ALLEN N. TOWNE

To Michele and Bob from Uncle Ben

McFarland & Company, Inc., Publishers
Jefferson, North Carolina, and London

Frontispiece: Sgt. Allen N. Towne preparing to leave for the States at Dolzandov (Dolní Žandov), Czechoslovakia.

Library of Congress Cataloguing-in-Publication Data

Towne, Allen N.
    Doctor danger forward : a World War II memoir of a
combat medical aidman, First Infantry Division / by Allen N.
Towne.
        p.   cm.
    Includes index.
    ISBN 0-7864-0661-5 (softcover : 50# alkaline paper) ∞
    1. Towne, Allen N.   2. World War, 1939–1945—Medical
care—United States.   3. World War, 1939–1945—Personal
narratives, American.   4. Emergency medical technicians—
United States—Biography.   5. United States. Army—
Biography.   I. Title.
D807.U6T69   2000
940.54'7573'092—dc21
[B]   99-42439
                                                                            CIP

British Library Cataloguing-in-Publication data are available

Manufactured in the United States of America

McFarland & Company, Inc., Publishers
    Box 611, Jefferson, North Carolina 28640
        www.mcfarlandpub.com

Contents

Contents

Preface

I have read many stories about the Vietnam War and how that war was devastating to the morale of the fighting men. The general impression is that the soldiers suffered so much in fighting an unpopular war that when they left the service they blamed their personal problems on the war. This bothers me because I have never heard any stories about the veterans of World War II who thought their problems were caused by their participation in the war.

I believe there were many soldiers in World War II who suffered more than those in the Vietnam War. The tour of duty in Vietnam was one year, whereas many of the men in World War II were involved for a much longer time and had less chance of surviving.

The thesis that because the Vietnam War was unpopular it affected the morale of the soldiers is hard for me to understand. Many who saw early and constant action in World War II had lost hope of coming back, but their spirits were kept alive by the elan of their unit. They still fought well at the end of three years of combat.

Perhaps the important difference between these two wars is that, in World War II, everyone realized you were in it until the war was over. The bond between men in a unit became strong because, in order to survive, you had to help each other, even if it meant the ultimate sacrifice.

When the first men came back to the United States after the European conflict was over, they were ignored by the public because the war was still on in the Pacific. Yet they did not complain. All they wanted to do was to forget about the war and get back to civilian life.

I believe all wars are bad, and all soldiers who participate in wars have similar problems. I also believe it is harder on the morale of the soldiers if they cannot see an end to their participation in the war unless they are killed or severely wounded. Furthermore, I don't believe the experience of war really changes a person. If they became drunks, it probably would have happened anyway. The drunks I saw were already drunks. The people who ended up as shell shock (anxiety state) cases were, in my opinion, susceptible to this in civilian life. There were thieves and murderers in the service as well as in civilian life.

One of the studies of World War II, Paul Fussell's book *Wartime* (Oxford University Press, 1989), gives the impression that we will never know the real story about the war. Perhaps this is true, but I would like to try to show what it was like to be in an army assault unit in World War II. I would like to show the horror, the living conditions, the endless battles and the fading of hope that you might survive. Mistakes were made, as they are made in all wars. But in spite of everything, there was pride in the unit and loyalty to the other soldiers, and I want to show this, too. People were both kind and cruel, and there was time for fun and laughter.

There is another reason for writing this. I was a soldier in the 1st Infantry Division, and I personally know the contributions and sacrifices the men of this division made during the war. I have never seen much written about the division by a member of the division. Perhaps this diary will help correct this.

I should mention that, originally, the diary was based on my company's daily morning report plus notes I made during those years. When I put it all together in a manuscript, it was a bare-bones diary with the dates and places of every move, but it did not go into great detail. This skeletal story was enhanced by other notes and recollections by myself and other members of my unit, notably sergeants Woods and McFarland. Later, when several young people read the rough manuscript, they did not believe we fought the French army in World War II. They really did not have a clear picture of World War II. I have added explanations of the battles to give the uninformed reader some background. Because my feelings and ideas have changed in the more than fifty years since this all happened, I have added comments that seem pertinent.

I have several objectives in writing this book. They are:

1. To show how the ordinary combat soldier lived in World War II;
2. To explain the feeling of elan that exists in some Army units;
3. To show how some divisions are exploited because of their superb performance in battle; and
4. To show how after several years of combat, a soldier's allegiance and reason to fight is his loyalty to his unit rather than patriotism.

One

Troubled Times

This is a true story of a soldier who served with a combat team of the 1st U.S. Infantry Division in World War II. While this is a story about war and describes what all-out war is really like, I have tried to add more of the personal element to this story. Along with the horror, the fright, the waste, the heroism and the hardships, there is the humor, the monotony and, above all, the contrasting of reactions different people have to living for years under stressful conditions. While some people may consider war as an adventure, it soon loses that luster and is regarded by most as living in hell.

This story encompasses the entire time the 1st Infantry Division (called the Big Red One) was in combat in World War II. During this three-year period, the division saw action in North Africa, Sicily and the mainland of Europe. A little background of the times will help to bring out the atmosphere of this troubled period. The economy of the United States had improved, but the effects of the Depression still lingered, and jobs, especially for the young people, were scarce. The minimum wage was 40 cents an hour, and many families lived on $16 a week.

The war in Europe started in September 1939, and by the end of June 1940, Hitler's armies had occupied much of Europe. The U.S. Congress voted for a military draft, and the registration day for the draft was October 16, 1940.

To most young Americans, involvement in this war was inevitable. Thousands enlisted in the regular Army in the fall of 1940, rather than wait to be drafted. Others, like me, enlisted to obtain enough savings to be able to afford to continue in school. It was difficult for college students to obtain work, and $16 per week did not go far toward tuition and books. Also, the benefits of a college education seemed unclear, when I found that chemists with a master's degree from Harvard (with five years' experience) were making only $25 per week.

I enlisted on October 16, 1940. I had just started my third year of college when I decided it would be a smart move. One advantage of enlisting over being drafted was that you could select the type of work and location. I selected an ordnance unit in Panama. However, I found out early that the Army had its own priorities. Because the 1st Infantry Division was to be brought up to fighting strength, I was placed into the medical battalion that was part of the 1st Infantry Division.

I suspect this military buildup was caused by the ominous news from Europe. The German air force had started massive air raids on Great Britain as a prelude to invading. The British army had lost so many men and so much equipment in its defeat in France, it was quite possible the German army would conquer Great Britain. Thus, the United States might soon need some trained divisions in order to protect itself.

In November 1940, I became a member of Company B of the 1st Medical Battalion. This was one of four companies in the battalion, which consisted of three collecting companies and a clearing company. The collecting companies' duty was to gather the wounded from the infantry regimental combat teams and, after administering first aid, send them back to the clearing company, which would in turn send them back to a field hospital. In combat, the wounded soldiers would first be treated at the battalion aid stations or in the collecting company aid station (which would be located from a quarter mile to two miles behind the infantry). The collecting companies had four or five doctors, 100 enlisted men and 12 ambulances. Company B was, for all practical purposes, part of the 18th Infantry Regiment, as was Company A part of the 16th Infantry Regiment and Company C part of the 26th Infantry Regiment.

A combat team normally had a complement of about 5,000 men. It would consist of an infantry regiment of about 3,000 men plus an artillery battalion, engineers and a medical company. The 18th Infantry Regiment had the 32d Field Artillery Battalion. The 26th Infantry Regiment had the 33d Field Artillery Battalion, and the 16th Infantry Regiment had the 7th Field Artillery Battalion. The division also had a heavy artillery battalion, the 5th Field Artillery Battalion. This was the oldest unit in the U.S. Army and dated back to the Revolutionary War.

The 1st Infantry Division, in peacetime, had been garrisoned in various parts of the country. The consolidation of the 1st Division began at Fort Devens, Massachusetts, in early 1941. Part of the division spent the winter of 1941 in practice landings on beaches near Buzzards Bay, New River, North Carolina, and in Puerto Rico. The following summer, practice landing maneuvers were held at Onslow Beach, North Carolina. In the fall of 1942, the entire division participated in the 1st Army maneuvers in North Carolina.

My first few months in the Army were quite a shock. Everyone was forced into a regimented life, and there was very little time to relax. We were kept busy with calisthenics before breakfast, close order drill, forced marches of 12 miles before lunch, hikes carrying others on litters and classes on first aid. Even though we were in the medical corps (and were not armed), we had to qualify with sidearms, rifle and submachine gun.

Later, the training got even more arduous, and we had full field marches (carrying a full pack) of up to 33 miles in one day. We also practiced wrapping ambulances and trucks in large canvases and floating them across lakes. All of this made you healthy. In six months, my weight went from 120 pounds to 150 pounds, and it was all muscle.

In the late spring of 1941, I was promoted to private first class, and was selected to attend a medical technicians' school at an Army hospital in Denver, Colorado. I went by railroad from Fort Devens to Fitzsimons General Hospital in Denver. While I was in transit, the Germans invaded Russia (June 22, 1941). No one thought the Russians could last very long against the German army and air force. General Marshall (who was the U.S. Army chief of staff) stated he thought it would be over in about ten weeks. How wrong he was.

At Fitzsimons Hospital, I had ten weeks of intensive medical training. For five weeks, we had class work on all phases of a medical technicians' work. The classes were conducted by the resident doctors. The second five weeks were spent working with the nurses in the various wards of the large military hospital. It was there that I had my first experience with patients dying. Two of the men under my care died that month. We also practiced drawing blood from each other so we would be prepared to give blood transfusions or plasma.

I got back to my company just in time to go on maneuvers in North Carolina. The maneuvers shocked the entire country because it showed that the U.S. Army was poorly equipped. Many of the units participating in the maneuvers did not have modern weapons. Some were even using wooden props to simulate guns.

The maneuvers ended in early December 1941, and we returned to Fort Devens. We arrived late in the evening of December 6, 1941. It had been a long, grueling ride on the trucks, jeeps and ambulances from North Carolina, and we were all cold and tired on that Saturday night. We were looking forward to a good night's sleep in a bed for the first time in months. After sleeping late, we would enjoy a carefree, lazy Sunday morning and eat our meals inside a warm building.

Two

Pearl Harbor

It was Sunday, December 7, 1941. As usual, I was up early but many of the men were still in bed when an announcement came over the radio that the Japanese navy had attacked Pearl Harbor and was bombing the Pacific Fleet. We were all excited. This surprise attack meant the U.S. was now at war with Japan. Because of a treaty between Germany and Japan, we might also be at war with Germany. Because the U.S. had only two army divisions ready for combat, and the 1st Infantry Division was one of them, we knew we would be in action early.

Most of us felt a little apprehensive about going to war, but a little eager in that it would be a new adventure. We probably would be going to strange and new places and, as for getting hurt, we thought that that only happens to others.

In early January 1942, we were alerted, and the entire 1st Infantry Division boarded trains and left Fort Devens during the night. The trains had the window shades drawn so that no one could see it was a troop train. After a five- or six-hour ride, we arrived at the Brooklyn, New York, port of debarkation and boarded amphibious assault transport ships. We left the port under the cover of darkness with a large destroyer escort. We were not told where we were going, and we felt that this was it. We would soon see action.

When daylight came, we were out of sight of land, and the convoy was headed in a southerly direction. However, no one would tell us where we were going. That night, we could see explosions and fires at sea. The sailors told us that U.S. oil tankers about ten miles away were being attacked by German submarines, and one had been hit and was burning. Our convoy was not attacked, and nobody seemed scared or concerned. The only inconvenience was that no one could smoke on deck after dusk. There was a blackout to prevent detection by the German submarines.

The troop transports were manned by a mixture of newly activated reserve crews and recently drafted sailors with a nucleus of experienced regular Navy men. The sea was a bit rough, and many of the soldiers and some of the sailors became seasick. I watched one sailor on deck throwing up into the wind. After the spraying he received, I was sure that the next time he would turn the other way. An older sailor, who was also watching, laughed and turned to me and said, "A new draftee."

After traveling all night, the fleet assembled a few miles offshore and prepared for an assault landing. Instead of going into action, we landed on Virginia Beach. We were part of a simulated enemy invasion force attacking the United States. Some U.S. Marine units were defending the area.

The large troop transports carried the landing craft used to carry us to shore. The landing boats had to be placed into the sea and made ready for us to board. All of this took a long time due to the inexperienced Navy crew. I was watching the crew take a light tank out of the hold with a crane. As they swung it over the side of the ship, the cables slipped and the tank fell overboard into the ocean. It just missed the tank landing craft that was alongside. It was fortunate no one got hurt.

We went ashore by climbing over the side of the troop transport and down rope cargo nets that served as rope ladders and into the old-type Higgins assault boats. These boats did not have the bow ramps that were on the newer landing craft. We then had a fast ride to shore. When the boat grounded on the beach, we had to climb over the side of the Higgins boat, jump into the waist-deep water, unload the chests containing medical supplies and wade ashore, carrying our heavy loads. We set up the aid station on the beach and waited until the exercise was over. After spending a cold night on the beach, we loaded onto trains and went back to Fort Devens.

We later learned that one objective of our landing operation was to act as a decoy to hide the departure of a troop ship. A converted British luxury liner (either the *Queen Mary* or the *Queen Elizabeth*) had taken a large force of troops (unescorted) to Australia. These soldiers later formed the Americal Division, which fought in the Pacific campaigns.

In February 1942, the division moved to Camp Blanding, Florida, for more maneuvers. I was promoted to corporal on April 21, 1942, and was sent on the advance detail to prepare the company at Fort Benning, Georgia, where the division was to engage in live ammunition maneuvers. It was at Fort Benning that I applied for an appointment to the Chemical Warfare Officer Candidate School.

At Fort Benning, we lived in the woods and never were in the main base. It became quite hot during this period, and swarms of flies were a big problem. They were all around our open latrines and garbage pits. This is probably the reason that a large part of the 1st Division became infected with amoebic dysentery. I came down with amoebic dysentery and paratyphoid fever on the troop train on the way to our next station, the Indiantown Gap Military Reservation located near Harrisburg, Pennsylvania. Upon our arrival at the base, the troop train was met by a fleet of ambulances, and I went directly to the station hospital along with hundreds of other 1st Division men. This must have given the Army a lot to think about. The 1st Division was

one of the two Army divisions that was ready to fight, and now it was crippled by sickness.

Indiantown Gap was a staging area used to prepare units for overseas
duty, so there was no doubt that we were soon going overseas. When I was
discharged from the hospital and returned to the company, I found I had
been transferred to the Indiantown Gap Base Operation. I had been accepted
for the Chemical Warfare Officer Candidate School but, because I was in the
hospital and not able to attend at that time, an alternate went in my place. I
would have to stay at Indiantown Gap until there was another opening. I knew
that the Army does not always follow through and I might be stuck on this
base for a long time, so I talked to a colonel in division headquarters who
assured me that if I went back to the division, I would get faster results. So I
transferred back to my old company.

Shortly afterwards, we were alerted for departure. We turned in all of
our equipment and sent all of our civilian clothes home. We divided what we
had left into essential and nonessential personal property. The essential property went into an "A" duffel bag, and the nonessential went into a "B" duffel
bag. The "A" bags were to go with us, and the "B" bags went to a warehouse
to be kept safe until we retrieved them when we got back to the United States.
I wonder if they are still there. I never did find out what the Army did with
the "B" bags.

On August 2, 1942, the entire division (less the advance detail) boarded
trains at the Indiantown Gap Military Reservation for the last trip in the
U.S.A. After an uneventful ride, we arrived at a dock in Newark, New Jer-
sey. When we detrained, we formed into companies and marched to waiting
ferry boats that transported the 18,000 men to a dock in New York City. As
the ferry boats approached the other side of the Hudson river, the imposing
skyline of New York was replaced by the looming shape of the *Queen Mary*
with its large gray funnels pointing upward to the darkening sky. The ship
was no longer the glistening white luxurious passenger liner but was now
somber in its new coat of battleship gray. As the ferry got nearer, the huge
bow towered over the ferry boat, making it look like a toy.

When the ferry boat docked, we collected our gear and debarked. Our
company took its place in the long lines to wait our turn to board the *Queen
Mary*. The lines moved slowly because they were loading by only four gang-
ways. The wait gave us the opportunity to study this immense ship. There
were many decks. It seemed like there were at least ten. The number of port-
holes was staggering. There must have been at least 1,000 on one side. As
we got closer to the edge of the dock, I noticed there was a large ship
lying on its side in the water next to the *Queen Mary*. It was the burned-out
hulk of the French passenger liner *Normandie*. It had been set afire by German saboteurs, and the firemen had poured so much water in it that it had
capsized.

We were so close to the *Mary* and it was so tall that it was hard to determine the layout of the upper decks. I could see the lifeboat deck, and it looked as if there were only 12 lifeboats on this side. Did that mean there were only 24 lifeboats for 18,000 men? I hoped there were more lifeboats and that they were very large.

Finally, it was our time to board. As we went up the gangway to enter the ship, the first sergeant would call out each man's last name. When the man answered with his first name and middle initial, a naval officer would allow the man to board. Then each platoon was given the location of where they were to sleep and stow their gear. Our platoon was given a location on E deck, and we were to report there. After lugging our heavy gear up and down many decks, we found our sleeping quarters. We had been assigned space down in the depths of the ship adjacent to the main boilers. The space had a gray steel floor and a very low steel ceiling about six feet in height. We were beneath an indoor swimming pool. It had to be the worst place on the ship.

We had just unloaded our gear (full field pack and duffel bag) when one of the ship's crew came by to instruct us how to make up our beds. In his hard-to-understand cockney accent, he told us to grab a piece of canvas from the pile in the corner. It was a hammock. We were to attach it to the two metal rings welded to the bottom of the swimming pool (our ceiling). The hammock was made up of a six foot by three foot piece of canvas, and on each end there were four ropes attached to a metal hook. When we set up the hammocks and tried to lie in them, we promptly fell out. The sailor said we would soon get used to them.

A short time later, another of the crew came by and gave each of us a meal ticket. This was to get us into one of the dining rooms at a specific time. We were told we must be waiting there at the specified time because we only had 15 minutes to eat, and if we did not get in at that time we would have to wait for the next meal. Because of the large number of soldiers aboard, we were to get only two meals per day. We noticed that our meal time was in about 15 minutes, so we left to find the dining room. It was one of the large, luxurious dining rooms except all the luxury had been removed and there were long tables with benches. The food was set out on each table, family style. We were told to pick up plates and utensils and start eating. It seemed like we had only started when a whistle blew, and we were told to take our plates, empty them and place the plates and utensils in a barrel and get out so the next group could eat.

After dinner, we went back to our sleeping area to see if we could sleep in the hammocks. This was not very successful so most of the platoon laid the hammocks on the steel deck. With our blankets and shelter half under us it was not too bad. We did not need a blanket on top because the heat from the boilers kept the area at about 80 degrees. Several of us decided we would find a better place to sleep the next night. We also figured that if the ship was hit by a torpedo, we did not want to be way down in the bottom of the ship on E deck.

In the morning after breakfast, the *Queen Mary* was ready to leave New York, and we went on deck to bid farewell to the U.S.A. It was quite a sight to see with all the huge buildings. As the Statue of Liberty and the skyline of New York slowly faded in the distance, I couldn't help but think, *How long before we come back and will we all come back."*

Soon, a group of destroyers arrived to escort the *Mary* and we increased speed and started on a zigzag course. It was a sunny day and the salt air was stimulating, so we decided to find a place to sleep. The best spot seemed to be the boat deck. Not only was it airy and cool in August but it had a wood deck that was much softer than the steel of E deck. We moved up to the boat deck.

While we had been busy doing this, some time had passed before I took a look at the ocean. When I looked around, I realized the destroyers were not with us, and we were alone on the open ocean. The escorts could not keep up with the *Mary* and we were to make the crossing to England alone.

We were told it was safe because the *Mary* could travel at 33 miles per hour, and there wasn't any submarine or any other boat that could travel that fast. Of course, there had to be a reason for the many 40-mm anti-aircraft guns on the top deck and the several 5-inch guns on the lower decks, as well as the 8-inch gun on the stern.

If anything did happen, I figured there would be a problem because there were not enough lifeboats for all the men. The ship had been built to carry about 2,000 passengers and, with over 18,000 soldiers on board, it was crowded. It would have been impossible to take care of all the men in so few lifeboats and rafts.

There was one large room on the *Mary* set aside for recreation. It could have been the main ballroom. Anyhow, some enterprising soldiers decided to make some money, and they set up a tremendous gambling casino. I don't know where they got the equipment. Perhaps from the crew. There were all types of card games and even a roulette table. I often thought the Army must have been involved because we were all given a partial payment of one $10 bill just as we left the base. We had no place else to spend it, and if anyone lost the first wager he had nothing left. When we left the *Mary*, one man had won about $100,000. That was a lot of money in those days.

I slept on the lifeboat deck for two nights, and it was very comfortable. On the last night, we were coming close to Iceland, and it was cold so I decided to go back down to E deck. However, I was saved from that steam-bath because I was put on guard duty on the bow of the ship. I really wasn't sure what I was looking for but, with alternating two hours of being cold while on guard and four hours in a nice warm place with unlimited hot coffee, it was not bad.

The next day we sighted Ireland. I was thrilled for it was the first time I had ever seen another country, except Canada. We proceeded to go north of Ireland and then went south between Scotland and Ireland. We passed many small capes, inlets and small islands and then went up the Firth of Forth in Scotland. We dropped anchor offshore from the port of Gourock, Scotland, on August 7, 1942. A fleet of small boats came out to meet us. We then collected our gear and waited in long lines to load onto the small boats. They ferried us ashore to a railroad station. Here, we loaded onto troop trains and went south by train to England. Along the way, the train would stop at railroad stations. We would detrain, and British women would serve us food. After a long, tiring train ride, we arrived at Tidsworth Barracks in southern England. Tidsworth Barracks was a permanent British army installation located near the city of Salisbury. It consisted of many old Victorian brick barracks, mess halls and other buildings.

The base mess halls served the basic British army food to all the troops. The first two days the meals seemed good but then, as most of the meals were lamb, the smell of old lamb got stronger and stronger. After a week, I knew what the smell of mutton was like and did not like it. Soon I could hardly go near the mess hall without getting a little nauseous. I lived on tea, bread and cereal for the remainder of the time at Tidsworth. To this day, I have difficulty eating lamb.

At this time, the 1st Division was the only U.S. Division in the European Theater of Operations. While we were in England, there were a few German air attacks in our area, but they were of little significance. However, one thing will always stick in my mind. When a few bombs started dropping nearby, an old British sergeant yelled out, "To the corners, lads. Jerry is overhead." That's where I learned that the corner of a building is the best place to be in a bombing raid.

When I went to London on pass, I could really see the terrible destruction from the German air raids during the London blitz.

The time spent at Tidsworth Barracks was really a transition period. The majority of men were kept busy with small maneuvers and re-equipping. I missed many of the maneuvers because I was put to work in the base hospital. I was working with a psychiatrist who was trying to find ways to prevent soldiers from avoiding duty by pretending they were sick (malingering). His method was to give them spinal taps. A spinal tap can be very painful and the pain can last for several days. After one of these, they would either snap out of it or they really were sick.

Late in September, we were alerted and went by troop train to Scotland, near Glasgow, where this diary, or odyssey begins. At this time, all units in the 1st Infantry Division were given code names. Company B, 1st Medical Battalion, was called "Doctor B."

Three

Maneuvers in Scotland

October 1–10, 1942. Corkerhill, Glasgow, Scotland

On October 1, 1942 our company was alerted for immediate departure. We were now an integral part of the 18th Infantry Regimental Combat Team. We were taken by truck from Tidsworth Barracks to a railhead and traveled by troop train to Glasgow, Scotland. We were to participate in landing maneuvers with the British navy. Our company spent the first night in Scotland sleeping in a warehouse that belonged to the Teachers Highland Cream Distillery. However, we were not able to sample any of their wares.

The 18th Infantry Combat Team was ordered to set up camp on a golf course in Corkerhill, Paisley (a suburb of Glasgow). It was a level area with a good grass cover. It was also close to a tram stop so it was easy to get to downtown Glasgow. We erected pyramidal tents, and although they did not have floors, they were clean and neat. Each tent held eight men, and every man had a folding canvas cot. We put our duffel bags and other gear on the dry ground under the cots and made ourselves at home. The entire combat team of about 5,000 men was set up in this area. For a few days, we thought we really had it made. We were in a nice town, and we could take a tram to Glasgow and visit the big city. Because we were the first American soldiers stationed in Glasgow, the people were very friendly.

While Glasgow had hardly been touched by German bombers, it was very involved in the war effort. Glasgow was the home of the important Clyde shipbuilding operations, which had built the *Queen Mary* and the *Queen Elizabeth* passenger ships and were now building warships. It was also an important port for the Murmansk convoys that brought supplies to the Russians via the dangerous Arctic route.

I talked to several American seamen who had just returned from a convoy to the Russian port of Murmansk. Murmansk is the largest ice-free port within the Arctic Circle and was the only Soviet port accessible to Allied military supply ships. The seamen said they had been on a freighter in a large convoy of Allied ships that were bringing munitions and other supplies to help the Russian army. The convoy was protected by many Allied warships, but they could not keep the convoy from being attacked by German submarines and even surface ships. As the convoy neared land, they were attacked by German torpedo planes and dive bombers. Their ship had been sunk by a German bomber, and they had been picked out of the water by another ship. They were very lucky because a man could live only a short time in those icy waters. They said many ships were sunk, and it was a miracle that any ships got through to help the Russians.

A few days later, the rains started and with it came colder weather. The golf course turned into a quagmire, and even inside my tent there were a few inches of water. I had to hang everything on the inside of the tent or lay it on the cot. When I went to bed, everything had to be hung up or piled over me on the cot. To get dressed, I had to stand on the cot. After I got my shoes on, I would step into the water that covered the ground inside the tent. When anyone had a pass and wanted to go to Glasgow, he would clean up and hire someone to carry him piggy-back to dry ground.

Our toilet facilities were also a problem. The Scots had made a large canvas enclosure and inside this they had a series of platforms. The platforms were about five feet off the ground, and under them there were a number of large, black iron pots. On the platforms, they had installed a toilet seat over the hole directly above each black pot. It was a roofless, open-air outhouse. As each day progressed, the toilets would be used by thousands of men and the pots would fill and, finally the contents would protrude through the toilet seat. If you forgot to go early or had to go twice, you would have to survey the situation carefully and pick the one least full. The pots were emptied each evening, except on weekends. By Sunday night, they were quite full, and it was better if you did not have to go on Sunday. It was quite a sight on Monday morning. It became so bad on one weekend that a desperate soldier hanged himself amid the mess. It was more than he could take. After that, the situation improved because the pots were emptied every day.

The living conditions were so bad, that we started to get an increase in the number of sick. This was of great concern to the commanders, because if a man was ill he would have to go to the nearest U.S. Army hospital and would be gone for a long time. We could not obtain replacements, and as they wanted every unit to be at full strength for the forthcoming operation, the men must be kept under their control. Because of this, Company B had to set up the 18th Infantry Combat Team Hospital. The hospital was set up in three large tents on the golf course. I was the only one in our company who had been trained in an Army hospital so I was given the task of setting up the procedures and running the operation. At the same time, I was promoted to sergeant.

In each tent we set up 24 cots. This was not like a conventional hospital because we only had a folding canvas cot and several blankets for each man. The men would have their own mess kits and personal gear with them. I had daily rounds with the doctors, and they told me what medication to give and

I took care of it. The most common medications were aspirin, codeine and penicillin. Penicillin was new at that time, and we only gave it by injection. The penicillin was used to treat gonorrhea, which was quite prevalent. We were lucky that most everyone was in good health or we would have had a space problem. We could accommodate about 60 or 70 men, and the hospital was full most of the time. While this kept me out of some of the maneuvers, it also kept me from seeing much of the countryside.

October 11, 1942. Corkerhill, Scotland

We were alerted for departure to an unknown destination. We first had to dismantle the hospital. All severely sick men were sent to the nearest military hospital. Then we had to get our own gear ready for the move.

October 12, 1942. Corkerhill, Scotland

We left Corkerhill at 0600 hours and marched to the railroad station and entrained at 0900 hours. We were not sure where we were going except it was to a seaport north of Glasgow. We arrived at a pier at Gourock (the port of Glasgow) at 1200 hours and boarded the British troop ship *Reina del Pacifico* at 1400 hours. We were to participate in intensive landing maneuvers with the 18th Infantry Combat Team, and this ship was our initial home.

Most of the men slept in hammocks slung from the ceilings. They were put up at night and taken down in the morning to make room in the cramped quarters. You had to take care not to fall out when you tried to get into it, and it took a bit of practice to stay in it when you were sleeping.

October 13–24, 1942. Aboard various British troop ships

The troop ships were based in Loch Fyne, near Inverray. Loch Fyne is one of the many inlets that extend into the west side of Scotland from the North Channel, which separates Northern Ireland from Scotland. Loch Fyne is north of Arran Island and about 60 miles west of Glasgow. The landing maneuvers were held on the beaches in Loch Fyne. This is rugged country, and we would go aboard other troop transports (the HMS *Ettrick* and the *Llangibby Castle*) and land with the infantry. This gave us practice climbing down the rope cargo nets while loaded with equipment. The nets were used as wide rope ladders, and we used them to board the much smaller assault landing boats that would be bobbing alongside the larger transports. We would have a fast ride to shore and, after the landing boats hit bottom, we would wade ashore onto unfamiliar terrain. Then we would hike for some miles inland and up hills in the ever-present rain. This is where I saw swamps or bogs on top of high hills. It rained so much that the water could not drain off. After a long march, we would hike back to the ships.

These maneuvers were to help all of the units of the combat team learn to work together on unfamiliar beaches and with a foreign navy. We learned to shake off the last ties of civilian life and became a well-oiled fighting machine. We also got plenty of exercise.

As the days went by, I noticed it was getting dark early and the days were getting very short. For the first time, I realized that Scotland is much farther north than Boston.

There were also some pleasant incidents amid all this hard work. One day, after a long maneuver in the damp waters and hills of western Scotland, we came back to the mother ship in the small assault boats. It was getting dark as we clambered aboard, and after a dinner of tea, bread and beef stew, I went on deck. A cool breeze gently caressed my face and the moon had risen to light up the blacked-out deck. Then I heard a British marine singing Irish songs in a wonderful tenor voice. The haunting melodies of "Danny Boy" and "Rose of Tralee" seemed to be magnified and filled the night. It was a fleeting moment of magic.

After the final maneuver, we stayed a few days at the U.S. Navy base at Roseneath, Scotland, where we slept in Quonset huts and had excellent U.S. Navy food. We were able to buy all types of American products at the Navy Post Exchange. They had many brands of candy, cigarettes and other luxury items. I call them luxury items because we had not been able to buy any American products in England or Scotland, and the British had none of these products for sale. I bought a case (96 cans) of Planters canned peanuts. Pvt. Randall, our jeep driver, put the case of peanuts on his jeep so it would be available wherever we went.

We had left all our vehicles and ambulances in the States and had been issued new ones here for the next operation. The vehicles were to be loaded on other ships along with the drivers.

After spending a pleasant time eating U.S. Navy food, we went back on the *Ettrick*, which was to be our home during the sea voyage to an unknown destination. The *Ettrick* was a rather new ship, having been built in Glasgow in 1938. The only modification that had been made was that the lifeboats had been replaced by landing craft. It was built to carry 1,254 troops and officers, but now it was carrying 2,500 officers and men. The entire 1st Battalion of the 18th Infantry plus support troops was on the ship. The *Ettrick* had five complete decks, which would help to make a long voyage more bearable because we could walk and exercise on the decks. I had to set up a dispensary, or hospital, on board the ship. Actually, there was a small hospital on the ship because it was a British troop ship, and we would operate the ship's hospital.

Four

The First Battle

October 25–26, 1942. Aboard the HMS Ettrick, *Roseneath, Scotland*

On October 25, supplies were loaded on the *Ettrick* and we knew we would soon be leaving. The food they were lowering in the hold did not look very appetizing. There were skinned carcasses of sheep and others that looked like rabbits. I did not see any refrigeration and hoped it was to be a short voyage.

At 2100 hours the next day, the *Ettrick* left the mooring, proceeded down the channels on the west coast of Scotland into the North Channel and then turned north. After a while we turned west toward open sea.

The first breakfast was a dismal meal. We had hot tea (by now we were used to tea), but we were not expecting a large, cold, black smoked herring and oatmeal for breakfast. Most of us just looked at the herring, shuddered and proceeded to eat the oatmeal until we discovered there were worms in it. They were dead worms, but it did not seem to make it more palatable. There was so much objection to the meal that all the food was taken away, and we had eggs and bread. The food was better afterwards. Maybe we got used to the food or the ship's cooks found a way to disguise the food, because I don't remember any more complaints. Perhaps it was the rum ration issued to all troops carried on British troop ships that made everything taste better. We were issued the same amount of rum given to the British seamen. The rum was a thick, dark Jamaican rum. It was very potent, and I had to mix it with water so I wouldn't burn my throat.

The *Ettrick* was a former British Pacific & Orient passenger ship. In the past, it had made trips to India and so there were a lot of Lashkars in the crew. Lashkars, who are natives of India, are either Hindus or Muslims. They have a peculiar ritual that confounded us. When they went to the toilet, they carried a full cup of water with them. We never could figure out what they did with the water, but it was a rigid ritual.

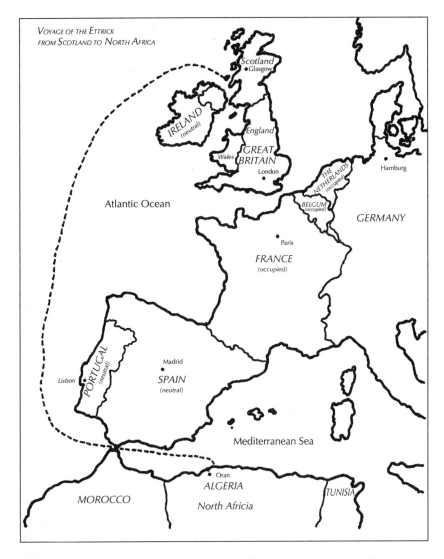

VOYAGE OF THE ETTRICK
FROM SCOTLAND TO NORTH AFRICA

Scotland
• Glasgow

IRELAND
(neutral)

England

GREAT
BRITAIN

Wales

London

THE
NETHERLANDS
(occupied)

Hamburg

Atlantic Ocean

BELGUM
(occupied)

GERMANY

• Paris

FRANCE
(occupied)

PORTUGAL
(neutral)

Madrid
•

Lisbon

SPAIN
(neutral)

Mediterranean Sea

• Oran

ALGERIA

MOROCCO

North Africia

TUNISIA

Route of the 18th Regimental Combat Team's Voyage from Rosneath, Scotland, to Arzew, Algeria.

October 27–November 10, 1942. At sea aboard the Ettrick

Other ships joined our little fleet, and we were now part of a large convoy of troop ships and warships heading south in the Atlantic Ocean. After a while, the convoy turned east, and then north and finally south again. We seemed to be going in a large circle. When the weather started to get warmer, we all tried to guess where we were heading. To Dakar? North Africa? Around Africa?

During the voyage, there were several submarine alerts. One time, the hostile submarines were very close, and the destroyers were racing around dropping depth charges. I wanted to stay on deck to watch, but we were told to go below deck. The depth charges really rocked the *Ettrick* and I could feel and hear the explosions as they went off. It was a bit scary but, as far as I could determine, none of the ships were hit.

When we finally were allowed back on deck, one of the small aircraft carriers escorting the convoy launched a plane to help in the submarine search. Instead of going up in the air, it dropped off the end of the carrier and plopped into the ocean. The last I saw, before the carrier was out of sight, were the destroyers racing around, searching for the pilot.

On the night of November 6, 1942, our convoy of troop ships and covering warships passed through the straits of Gibraltar. We did not see Gibraltar because it was blacked out. However, we did see a glow of lights on our left. This would be the Spanish mainland. Later, lights on the right were seen. They were the lights of Tangiers, Morocco. We were now in the Mediterranean Sea.

The next morning, we were out of sight of land. Soon, the troop ship changed course and, after a while, far in the distance, I could see a faint ribbon of land as it emerged from the sea. As the ship got closer, I had my first look at North Africa. I was disappointed because it was not exotic or unusual. The coastal area sloped up into low hills. There was not much vegetation, although I could see some palm trees. On the whole, it was a bit drab.

All of us were worrying and wondering if we would have more intense German and Italian submarine activity and perhaps air attacks as we proceeded along the coast of North Africa. We were not very far from German and Italian military installations. We now knew that we were to land in the vicinity of Oran, Algeria. This was Vichy French territory, and the French might resist an American landing. We were not sure what sort of a reception we would get from the French in North Africa. We were told there was a good chance there would not be any resistance, but we were not sure what would happen.

On November 8, 1942, we were offshore near Oran, Algeria. Our convoy had been reinforced by two British warships, the HMS *Rodney* and the aircraft carrier *Furious*. Now the force consisted of the entire 1st Infantry Division and the 1st Ranger Battalion on 11 troop transports. This force was covered by the HMS *Rodney*, three aircraft carriers, three anti-aircraft cruisers, 13 destroyers and six other, smaller warships (all British). The 1st Infantry Division (reinforced by the 1st Ranger Battalion) was carried on the British troop ships: HMS *Royal Ulsterman*, HMS *Ulster Monarch*, HMS *Royal*

Scotsman, HMS *Reina del Pacifico,* HMS *Tegelberg,* HMS *Ettrick,* HMS *Warwick Castle,* HMS *Duchess of Bedford,* HMS *Monarch of Bermuda,* HMS *Glengyle* and HMS *Llangibby Castle.*

Later, the convoy split up. The ships carrying the main part of the division went close to Oran. The troop ships carrying the 18th Infantry Combat Team went north of Oran, and about midnight, stopped at their designated spots about five miles from the port of Arzew, Algeria. The ships' crews' worked hard to get all the landing craft lowered into the water. Then, the first assault teams loaded into the boats.

This was our first action, and we all were apprehensive, so we were up early to watch the initial attack by the 1st Ranger Battalion. At first, we thought the landing was unopposed, but we soon saw the red tracers from the machine guns. Then we knew the French had decided to fight. The 1st Ranger Battalion assaulted the docks at Arzew at 0500 hours, and the 18th Infantry landed south of the town. By 0900 hours, the port of Arzew and the surrounding area was in our hands except for occasional sniper fire.

The *Ettrick* tried to go in and unload at the dock in Arzew but, as we came in close to the dock, some enemy shells landed near us. One even hit the ship but did not explode. The *Ettrick* quickly backed out to a safe distance. We would have to go ashore in the small assault boats. We had to climb down the rope cargo nets while loaded with equipment to board the much smaller craft that were bobbing up and down alongside the larger transport. We had a fast ride to shore and, after the landing boat hit shore, we waded ashore onto Z beach, green, at Arzew, Algeria.

We left the *Ettrick* after being on board for 16 days. I learned later that the *Ettrick* was sunk by a German submarine on November 15, 1942, shortly after it passed through the straits of Gibraltar on its return voyage to England. The *Warwick Castle,* another ship that had carried part of the 1st Division to Africa, was sunk at the same time.

After landing, we collected and treated casualties and sent them to a field hospital being set up in Arzew. We did not have any vehicles ashore for a few days, so all we had for medical supplies was what we could carry in our large vest haversacks. These contained dressings, sulfa powder, morphine syrettes, bandages and other supplies.

One of the first wounded infantrymen I worked on had a small bullet hole in the front where it entered his shoulder. When it left his body, it had flattened out and ripped a 6- or 8-inch-diameter hole in his back. The bullet did a lot of damage. Billy Edwards, an aid man who was with me, was very nervous and excited. He was about to pour some pure alcohol in the gaping wound when I stopped him. He had forgotten what to do with a bad wound. I pushed him aside and poured on sulfa powder, and because the wound was so large, put on several dressings. Then I secured the dressings with a bandage. There were no vital parts hit, but it probably was a long time before the man was back in action. He was in a lot of pain so I gave him a shot of morphine. We used throwaway syrettes that contained a half grain of morphine.

The town of St. Cloud was the combat team's objective, and it was about eight miles away. There were very few vehicles ashore so we were all walking on the only road to St. Cloud. We did not know what to expect, and the infantrymen kept yelling that there were snipers on the hills on both sides of the road to St. Cloud. This first battle was both exciting and frightening. It got very hot, and the men were continually discarding gear. The sides of the road were littered with empty tin cans (used C rations), items of clothing and even gas masks.

While on this march, an old French warplane flew over very low. We did not have any anti-aircraft protection so a rifle company shot at it with rifles and machine guns. As unbelievable as it sounds, they shot it down. It was a long time before we had any U.S. Army anti-aircraft protection, although later we did get protection from British 40-mm anti-aircraft units.

While we were on our way to St. Cloud, we were supposed to be under sniper fire from the enemy on the hills on both sides of the road, but I did not see any snipers or results of sniper fire. While all of this might only have been a rumor, it made me realize that this was for real, and you could get killed in this action. We had already collected some of our own dead infantrymen.

We set up our collecting station about one mile from St. Cloud. It was here that the first serious resistance was encountered. Some units of the French Foreign Legion had set up a defensive position in St. Cloud. They were able to stall the advance of the 18th Combat Team through St. Cloud to Oran.

St. Cloud was on the main road to Oran and was a town of about 4,000 people. It was set in the middle of a little valley and was in the open with no trees or vegetation around it. The houses were made of brick and stone, which provided a great defense against small arms. The defenders of the town had a clear view in all directions, so an attacking force could incur heavy casualties unless it had tanks to aid in the attack. The 18th Infantry tried to take the town but was met with heavy rifle and machine gun fire. Because the artillery and tanks were not ashore it was decided to wait and renew the attack the next day, when artillery would be available.

That evening, because our vehicles had not yet landed, we used a captured truck to go closer to St. Cloud and evacuate casualties. We treated and evacuated casualties from the 18th Infantry, the 32 Field Artillery and the 1st Ranger Battalion. We sent them to the U.S. field hospital in Arzew.

As we came back from our night trip to the edge of St. Cloud, we passed a small group of the 1st Ranger Battalion who said they were going to take St. Cloud that night. Later we did hear a lot of firing, but it soon was quiet.

That night, everyone was on edge because it was our first action. The infantry companies had set up guard points, and if anyone approached them, they would challenge with the password "Hi Ho Silver." The proper response was "Away. Away." If you did not give the proper countersign, the guards would shoot. It was not expected that the French had ever listened to "The Lone Ranger" program on the radio. During the night, I heard a guard shouting, "Hi Ho Silver," and a few shots were fired. The next morning, we found a dead white horse in a nearby ditch. One of our men commented, "The Lone Ranger has been here and his horse Silver was killed." We all had a good laugh.

At 0700 hours the next morning, after a 15-minute artillery barrage, the 18th Infantry attacked St. Cloud without the support of tanks. The defenders were able to answer with heavy small arms fire. Without support from tanks, we would have many casualties.

The combat team commander asked for permission to use a 30-minute heavy concentration of artillery, including large 155-mm guns. The division commander refused because there were so many civilians in the town. The 18th Infantry was then ordered to bypass the town and leave a battalion to keep the French Legionnaires in place.

We marched with the main force toward Oran. The resistance was spotty, and we kept going until we met other units of the 1st Division, who had landed on the other side of Oran, and the large seaport was surrounded.

By 1000 hours on November 10, 1942, all fighting was over in Oran, and by noon an armistice was in effect. St. Cloud did not surrender until the French high command in Oran surrendered all the French troops in the area.

We moved the aid station into St. Cloud at 1800 hours and started to clear the little town of all the wounded and dead. Our first concern was the wounded. There were not many wounded left in the town, and in a short time, we had treated and evacuated all them. While most of the wounded were American soldiers, there were some civilians and a few French Foreign Legionnaires.

The Legionnaires, who were the enemy, had come from their big barracks in nearby Sidi-Bel-Abbès to defend St. Cloud and to prevent the 18th Infantry from attacking Oran from the north. A few of the Legionnaires were being held as prisoners in the central square, where we had set up our aid station. The Legion was somewhat like a mercenary army and would fight any other army when given the order by their commanders. They were excellent soldiers.

Ordinarily, a medical unit would not have to remove the dead, but in North Africa there were no U.S. Army units to do this, and as we had the litters, personnel and ambulances, we were given the task. We were following some Arab civilians, who were leading us to a place where there were dead Americans, when we came into a narrow street, really an alley between some buildings, and saw a horrifying sight.

There were nine American soldiers lying dead in the alley. They had come under machine gun fire from an ambush by soldiers of the French Foreign Legion. They were lying in various positions, and it looked as if it had taken some of them a long time to die. One had his water canteen in his hand, as if he were ready to drink. Another soldier was lying on his back with his hand frozen by rigor mortis, holding rosary beads over his eyes. He must have been praying as he lay dying. Others were still clutching their weapons as they died. This was what was left of the small group of the 1st Ranger Battalion we had seen two nights ago when we had been picking up the wounded on the outskirts of St. Cloud. Their bodies had been lying there almost two days, and the sweetish, sickening odor of human dead hung over the area. We all stopped quickly, and a collective gasp went up as we took in the scene. A few men just turned away. I could feel the blood drain from my face. I turned cold and felt a few shivers run up my body. The smell was what bothered me and for a few seconds I thought I was going to be sick.

I pulled myself together, and along with the rest of the men, started to pick up the bodies. This was a bit difficult as we had to strip the weapons and other gear from their bodies, which were stiff from rigor mortis. One of our men, who had started to help in the removal of the dead soldiers, turned very pale. He then started to shake and finally started to cry and scream. When we tried to quiet him down, he got violent, and we had to restrain him. Finally, we gave him a shot of morphine. This quieted him down, and we sent him back to the evacuation hospital. This really sobered everyone and gave us a lot to think about. Was this what was called shell shock in World War I? Could this happen to us?

We resumed our work with the bodies, recorded their names, serial numbers and units, put the bodies in mattress covers and sent them back to a collection point.

This incident preyed on our minds for quite a while and, later that evening, another man who had participated in the removal of the dead bodies started trembling and crying, and shortly we had another man who had to be restrained and sedated. This time, we took the man to the U.S. Army hospital that had just been set up in the city of Oran. We never saw these men again as they were eventually sent back to the States. We also were given a new name for this condition. It was not to be called shell shock but "anxiety state." We knew we would probably see more of it before this war was over.

The first taste of action is not easy, and everyone is scared. We were lucky it did not last long. We also found that some people cannot cope with the results of violence. In battle, you have to make a personal adjustment about the values of life and death or at least put it in the back of your mind or you can lose control of yourself.

November 11, 1942. St. Cloud, Algeria

All our vehicles had now been unloaded from the ships, and we were able to set up the complete aid station and take care of the remaining minor casualties. The aid station consisted of four large cases, each the size of a trunk. These cases carried many of the essential medical supplies and instruments, splints, sterilizers, etc. The cases, when set on end in pairs placed about six feet apart, would be a platform for a litter and enable a doctor and aid men to work on a wounded man. We also carried large canvas cases of blankets. These were needed because many wounded men go into shock and need to be kept warm. We carried other medical supplies but this was the essential setup. Because the weather was mild, we set up the aid station in the open rather than in the large tent that we carried. We now were evacuating to the hospital in Oran.

We had two men in our company wounded in the three day action. Pvt. Donald Hutchinson (gunshot wound, right thigh), and Pvt. William Doherty (shrapnel wound, left shoulder). Both had been evacuated to the 48th Evacuation Hospital, Arzew.

November 12, 1942. Oggaz, Algeria

We left St. Cloud at 0800 and went by truck to Oggaz. We arrived at 1200 hours. Because we were not sure that we were to stay, we bivouacked. This means we did not set up camp. We just pulled off the road and slept on the ground near the vehicles.

November 13–27, 1942. Oggaz, Algeria

A decision was made to set up our permanent camp at Oggaz. We were to camp near the other companies of the 1st Medical Battalion and not with the 18th Infantry. However, three of our ambulances and drivers stayed with the 18th Infantry Battalion for evacuation of the sick.

We all set up our pup tents. Because every man carries only one half of a tent, it takes two men to set up one tent. I set up mine with Cpl. McFarland. We each had our own blanket and used our raincoats as doors when it rained. These tents did not have door flaps.

The large tent was set up and used as a dispensary for men of our company. It was also used as the company headquarters. The company cookstoves were set up and operating. We had only canned C rations so the cooks warmed up the cans. They also provided hot water for our instant coffee and to wash our mess kits.

Our water trailer was filled with purified water from the division water point, and a slit trench latrine was set up nearby. We got into the routine of washing and shaving using the steel part of our helmets as wash basins. We would also use the helmets to wash socks and underwear. Because we only had one set of clothes, we would exchange them for clean uniforms when we went to the portable shower units that were set up nearby.

We had to check our equipment and replenish our supplies, so we would be ready for the next operation.

I was able to retrieve my case of peanuts from the jeep driver. He had only eaten a few cans, so I had plenty to give away and for trading. They tasted good after the long period of British rations.

We also received mail from home. We hadn't had mail for about a month, and there was a lot of mail and even some packages.

Some of us tried swimming and washing in the Mediterranean and found it to be quite cool in late November. However, in the day it was nice and warm. The weather was one thing that surprised me. I had expected that Africa would be hot. It could get hot in the day, if the sun was out. We were coming into the rainy season, and we had an increasing number of cloudy days. At night it would get quite cool. We had an advantage over the other soldiers because the medical units carried a lot of blankets, whereas all others had only one. This is where I learned that the two-man pup tents could be kept warm by burning a small candle in the tent.

We were able to get passes to go to the city of Oran and other nearby towns. Oran is quite a large city and is a mixture of European and African cultures. It sits on a steep slope of a small mountain (Jebel Murjajo) and is divided by a ravine. The old section is west of the ravine, and the newer section is on the east side. The newer part has wide, palm-lined streets, wide sidewalks and modern buildings. A lot of Europeans lived in this area. The other section is built on the steep hill and has very narrow streets and alleys between buildings. These alleys have stairs so you could go from one street up or down to another street. This section is where most of the Arabs lived and also where much of the large Jewish population resided. One of our men was able to speak Yiddish, and we found that many of the Jewish people had fled from Germany via Spain and France. The Arab women wore robes with part over their heads and seemed to always have one eye covered.

It was in Oran that I saw the motion picture *Yankee Doodle Dandy* with French subtitles. I also saw a stage show (from Paris), The Folies-Bergère, and Josephine Baker, a black American-born singer.

The people in Algeria were unable to obtain gasoline for their cars and trucks, so they adapted their carburetors to use alcohol. Algeria has a lot of vineyards and produces quite a bit of wine. The wine was distilled down to almost pure alcohol and used to run their vehicles. One of the distilleries (a rather rustic one similar to a moonshiners' stills) was nearby. In our company, we had an alcoholic named Smith. He went over to this distillery and found a 500-gallon vat full of wine alcohol and started drinking it, using his helmet as a cup. He had to reach way down to get the alcohol and, after some time, he became unsteady. He finally fell in the vat and almost drowned. He was lucky that one of our men heard him yelling. He had to be pulled out. Perhaps it would have been a blissful way for him to die.

I was in the small town of Oggaz one day, and I saw three very old Arabs sprawled against an old building. Then I noticed that one was not an Arab because he was dressed in a U.S. Army uniform. It was Smith. He did not have a hat, and he had lost his false teeth. He had been drinking and passed out next to the two Arabs. We had him picked up and brought back to the company area. He didn't stay with the company much longer.

It seemed to me that the French people had the automobiles in Algeria, and the Arabs used donkeys. They called them *ans*. These donkeys were very small with little skinny legs. When an Arab would ride one, his legs would almost drag on the ground. They would put immense loads on these little animals, but nothing seemed to bother them.

November 28–30, 1942. St. Barbe de Thelot, Algeria

The company moved from Oggaz at 0800 hours on the 28th to a new bivouac area. We were now back in an assembly area with the 18th Infantry. It was rumored that we would soon be moving to Tunisia. During this wait, we heard that there had been a bad fire at the Coconut Grove in Boston and hundreds had died. Many of us were from the Boston area, and the stories going around would make you think that everyone you knew had died in the fire. By the time we did get any real information on the fire, we were too involved to read about it.

We also had time to reflect a bit on our first taste of war. While it had only lasted three days, it was full of confusion, fear and uncertainty. I had not realized that a landing on a hostile shore is one of the most difficult and confusing operations. I hoped the next action would be easier.

The 1st Division had suffered a total of 418 casualties in this three-day operation. There were 94 killed, 73 seriously wounded, 178 slightly wounded and 73 missing.

December 1–6, 1942. St. Barbe de Thelot, Algeria

We now had other things to think about. We knew the British 1st Army had landed farther east at Algiers and was trying to reach Tunis in force before the Germans brought in reinforcements. It was apparent we would soon be in this battle because some of the division units had already been committed in Tunisia.

December 7, 1942. St. Barbe de Thelot, Algeria

Our company was alerted at 1700 hours to prepare to move with the 18th Infantry Combat Team to an unknown destination. The company was to be ready to move at 2100 hours from Oggaz. Men who were absent or in the hospital were transferred to Company A of the 1st Medical Battalion, and six men from the headquarters company were transferred to our company as replacements.

The company was waiting to move and did not get to Oggaz until after 12 midnight. Then we left at 4:30 in the morning for L'Arba. We were parked on a road.

Five

With the British Army

December 8, 1942. Oggaz, Algeria

The company left Oggaz at 0430 hours to join the 18th Infantry Combat Team. When we arrived at the assembly point, our vehicles were given a place in the column and the long convoy headed east for an unknown destination. The weather was cloudy and it looked like rain. The roads were excellent. When night came, we had to follow the vehicle ahead very closely because we could not use the regular headlights. We had to use our blackout lights, little slits of blue light that could only be seen from a short distance.

It began to rain, making the visibility even worse. The convoy moved very slow. We drove steadily until 2300 hours. When we stopped for the rest period, we just pulled over to the side of the road and tried to sleep the best we could. Because it was raining heavily, most of the men slept in the vehicles, and it was extremely uncomfortable.

December 9–14, 1942. L'Arba, Algeria

We arrived in L'Arba, Algeria (near Algiers), after traveling 300 miles in the long convoy of military vehicles. We bivouacked in a grove of cork trees. These trees were about 50 feet tall and had large trunks. Some of them had the bark peeled off, a spongy, somewhat elastic layer that was several inches thick. Harvesting cork was a big business in this area. It was a pleasant place to stay for a few days. We had good cover and did not have any problem with enemy aircraft.

The 1st Platoon of Company B, 1st Engineer Combat Battalion (part of the 18th Combat Team) was attached to our company for rations and administration. The platoon consisted of one officer and 43 men. The combat team was waiting for orders, and our ambulances were evacuating sick from the 18th Infantry Combat Team to a hospital in Algiers.

27

December 15, 1942. Sétif, Algeria

We left L'Arba at 1100 hours and traveled 218 miles to Sétif, where we bivouacked for the night. It was hard going because the roads were not very good. The long convoy of vehicles did not travel very fast, and there were frequent stops. It took a long time to gas up because we had to use 5-gallon cans to refuel the vehicles.

December 16, 1942. Constantine
(20 miles east), Algeria

We left Sétif and traveled 190 miles to a location 20 miles east of the ancient Roman city of Constantine. Constantine is a fairly large city and is the capital of the Algerian department of Constantine. Most of the traveling was done at night because of German air activity. They had control of the air and could cause a lot of damage because we had very little anti-aircraft protection.

We bivouacked for the night near a railroad switchhouse. Cpl. McFarland and I went over to the switchhouse, where we found several French railroad men drinking wine. They were very sociable and offered us some wine, and we had a good conversation and even sang the "Marseillaise" with them. I am not sure any of us knew what the other was talking about. They couldn't speak English, and my French was not very good. The conversation ended when the wine ran out.

December 17–19, 1942. Ghardimaou, Tunisia

We left the area near Constantine and traveled 190 miles to Ghardimaou. This was a British 1st Army staging area. We must have been near a battle zone because the British had tight security in the area.

This type of travel was hard on everyone. A combat team consists of about 5,000 men, and with all the equipment, guns and supplies, there are many vehicles involved and any breakdowns cause long delays. To make matters worse, the weather was cold and rainy, and at night the visibility was poor. It was very tiring sitting in the trucks and ambulances. When we did stop, most of the men would roll themselves up in their shelter half (½ tent) and sleep on the ground in the rain.

December 20–21, 1942. Guatamala, Tunisia

Here we had to wait for combat orders. We were now attached to the British 1st Army and were part of the British V Corps.

December 22–23, 1942. Medjez-el-Bab, Tunisia

The British 1st Army, after landing near Algiers, had tried to get to Tunis before the Germans. The British along with elements of the U.S. 1st Armored Division, had been able to get close to Tunis but, because of bad roads, bad weather and lack of experienced troops, had not been able to keep to their timetable. In the meantime, the Germans had landed airborne troops and were bringing in heavy tanks by sea. By the end of November, the Germans had 15,000 troops in the Tunis, area as well as 81 fighter planes and 28 Stuka dive bombers. These were followed by three more German divisions and two Italian divisions.

The British were forced to fall back into the mountains to the west of Tunis. The British Coldstream Guards had taken a vital hill (called Longstop Hill) near the main road from Medjez-el-Bab to Tunis. This position was to be taken over by the 18th Infantry's 1st Battalion.

Our company bivouacked near Medjez-el-Bab. On December 23, the aid station and some litter bearers (25 men and two doctors) went forward with the 1st Battalion of the 18th Infantry. The remainder of the company left Medjez-el-Bab and went to Teboursouk and bivouacked. They would send meals up to us in the aid station.

The 18th took over some of the Coldstream Guards' positions on Longstop Hill in a driving rain storm. A short time later, the Germans counterattacked, and some of the positions were lost. The 18th Infantry then counterattacked to try to regain them. During this action, the aid station was receiving both American and British casualties.

December 24–25, 1942. Medjez-el-Bab, Tunisia

On Christmas eve, the 1st Battalion of the 18th and the Coldstream Guards made another assault on Longstop Hill but not all of the hill was retaken.

On Christmas day, the Germans launched a fierce counterattack using a superior force that included the huge Tiger tanks that had 88-mm guns. We only had little 37-mm anti-tank guns to use against the Tiger tanks. The shells just bounced off the German tanks. The 18th Infantry and the Coldstream Guards could not hold out against the Germans, and the strategic hill was lost. The 18th fell back to defensive positions, dug in and prepared for new German attacks.

Our aid station was very busy during this three-day battle. The work was made difficult because it had rained steadily, and the weather was cold. Our aid station was evacuating casualties from both U.S. and British units to a British army hospital. We were so busy with the flood of wounded that we did not realize it was Christmas.

The 18th Infantry had 350 men killed, wounded or missing, and the Coldstream Guards lost 200 men in this action. We were not able to collect all of our dead because the area was now in German hands.

This is how the 18th Infantry Combat Team spent its first Christmas overseas.

December 26, 1942. Teboursouk, Tunisia

The aid station and litter bearers left the immediate battle area and rejoined the rest of the company at Teboursouk. The aid station was set up and in operation.

December 27–29, 1942. Teboursouk, Tunisia

The aid station was treating casualties, and the ambulances were still evacuating to British hospitals. The situation was quite fluid and confusing. Because of this, there was a great deal of security, with many roadblocks and outposts. At night, it was dangerous to go far unless you were sure of the password. One night, two British officers were out in a jeep with a driver and, when they were challenged at a British roadblock, they gave the wrong countersign. The sentry opened fire at point blank range with a Thompson submachine gun. When we got the three wounded men back to our aid station, there was little we could do. In a short time, all three died.

We did have Christmas music and gossiping chatter on the radio. I had a portable radio. It was a bit large, compared to present-day portables, and had a range of about 75 miles. I managed to bring it overseas, and a friend in the Signal Corps kept it in repair and supplied with batteries. I paid him with cans of my valuable peanuts. I was able to tune into the German propaganda broadcasts from Tunis. They featured a girl who talked about the war in English and played American songs. We called her "Gertie from Bizertie." She talked about the battle of Longstop Hill and mentioned the names of some of the 18th Infantry men who were captured by the Germans during this battle. She said we were losing the war and should give up.

December 30–31, 1942. 4 miles from
Medjez-el-Bab, Tunisia

We left Teboursouk and went back to Medjez-el-Bab and set up the aid station in our old position. Here, we had more protection from shelling and from air attacks. There was a great deal of German air activity, and more anti-aircraft protection was needed in the area. Finally, an American anti-aircraft unit set up in the vicinity. Because it was a small group and did not have a kitchen truck, 15 men from the 431st CAA (anti-aircraft) were attached to our company for rations.

One German plane had been shot down in the area, and some of our men salvaged the Plexiglas windshield and carved rings and medallions from the Plexiglas.

January 1–10, 1943. Medjez-el-Bab (6 miles southwest), Tunisia

The aid station was moved to a sheltered area to protect it from air raids and shelling. We set it up in a large culvert where it could not be seen from the air and it was almost impossible for a shell to hit it.

Because the German air force had control of the air, we had to be careful in our vehicle movements. One time the jeep driver and I went to the Company B, 1st Engineer Battalion's water point. This is where the drinking water was purified. We filled a few five-gallon cans and were coming back to the aid station when a German plane came over very low to strafe. The jeep driver jammed on the brakes and stopped short. The water cans, which were behind me in the jeep, flew over my head onto the road. It's a wonder I was not decapitated. The plane was so low I could see the pilot with a cigarette in his mouth. After I stopped shivering, I picked up the water cans, and we went back to the aid station.

Another time, I went in the jeep to pick up some medical supplies from the British. On the way back, we saw an Arab carrying a basket of eggs. We stopped and bartered for them. Finally, the Arab traded the eggs for some C rations and coffee. The jeep driver, Cpl. Randall, got out his mess kit and some cooking oil. Using an empty C ration can partly filled with gasoline as a stove, we cooked and ate 65 eggs. They were small eggs, but they were good.

January 11–31, 1943. Medjez-el-Bab (6 miles southwest), Tunisia

The collecting station was moved to a farmhouse, and we occupied two rooms. We did this so we could hold men who were slightly wounded or sick until they were well enough to go back to duty. If a man was sent back to a hospital, he would go to a British hospital and be gone for a long time, and replacements were difficult, if not impossible, to obtain. The 18th Infantry had lost a lot of men and needed every man.

We even had British soldiers in our little hospital. Most of the men held here had infections such as severe boils and carbuncles on the neck or a superficial wound that had become infected. We would lance the swollen, infected portion and insert a gauze drain soaked in alcohol. We would make sure the wound or infection was kept clean and change the drain as required. The infantry-men were living in covered holes and were not able to really wash, and this no doubt contributed to the increase in infections.

Some of the problems could have been caused by improper food. We had been on British rations since December 20. While it was adequate, we were not used to it and probably did not eat all of the rations so as to get a balanced diet. The basic beverage was tea. It was good, but many men did not like tea. The rations contained hard biscuits and very good jam. The rest of the food was not very appetizing. It consisted of canned steak and kidney pudding, oxtail stew, etc. As a result of this diet, most of us had sore gums, and we craved fresh foods. Many of us were eating raw onions. We would eat them as if they were apples. I even got to like limes and would peel a lime and eat it as if it were an orange. These were native onions and limes we got from the Arabs.

One time, the 18th Quartermaster Unit obtained some U.S. Army rations, and we had a banquet on canned chili con carne, coffee and canned peaches with evaporated milk. In the aid station, which was apart from the rest of the company, we had a kitchen stove to keep the aid station warm. One time, we found some potatoes in the barn and got some lard from the Arabs and had deep-fried potatoes until the lard got used up. We felt we were living like kings. The infantry-men on the lines did not have the opportunity to get as much fresh food from the Arabs as we did, so they got more infections.

On January 25, the company area was strafed by enemy aircraft and shelled by their artillery. One of our men (Pvt. Glenn Addison) was slightly wounded (shell fragment, left leg). He was treated at the aid station and returned to duty.

The manpower situation was so bad that some of our men were asked to help repair roads. In one extreme situation, a few of our men volunteered for outpost duty in a quiet area.

February 1, 1943. Medjez-el-Bab
   (6 miles southwest), Tunisia

We were jarred awake the night of January 31 by a tremendous barrage of mortar fire and heavy machine gun and rifle fire. The sky was lit up by phosphorus flares suspended by little parachutes and the battle continued for several hours. It was some time before we knew what was going on but then we received orders to send three ambulances and some litter squads to the 2nd

Battalion of the 18th Infantry. There were both German and American casualties resulting from a skirmish with a large German patrol that entered our positions at night. The German patrol was captured (less the ones killed).

It was in this action that the combat team had the first taste of German dirty tricks. Several of the Germans were in an impossible situation and put up their hands to surrender. When several of the 18th Infantry men went up to them, one of the Germans pulled out a concealed machine pistol and killed the Americans. The news of this action spread through the combat team, and no one will be caught by this trick again. We treated and evacuated both our own and the German wounded.

February 2–12, 1943. Medjez-el-Bab (6 miles southwest), Tunisia

The horrible living conditions were getting worse for the infantrymen. They were living in this cold wet weather, sleeping in covered holes to protect them from shell bursts. They had not changed their clothes for months. They never took off their clothes at night because you never know when you might have to get up quickly and, besides, you need your clothes for warmth. You always had to make the big decision each night. Should I take my shoes off? It was more comfortable to sleep with your shoes off, but if you had to get up quickly, you would rather have them on. You also wanted to keep your blanket as clean as possible, so you would not want to have dirty, wet, shoes in your blanket. Or, if you had just come into a new area and were really dog tired and were to move out soon, you would wrap yourself up in the blanket and a shelter half and lie down in the mud with the rain coming down.

Even the simple things, like washing your face, became a chore. We each had one washcloth and one towel. They were olive drab and did not show the dirt. The wash cloth would get mildew and smell bad and so would the towel. Many times, you would just wipe the grime off rather than wash it off. The washcloth and towel would be set out in the sun (whenever the sun was out) and dried as well as possible. When dry, you would shake it hard to remove the dirt.

We used the steel part of our helmet as a washbasin and, if we were near a cook stove, we could obtain a little hot water. If not, the men would take a little gasoline and pour it into an empty ration can, light it and heat up a little water in their canteen cups. Some men started to grow beards because they figured it would be easier to take care of a beard than to shave. I started a beard but I soon found out that it was harder to keep clean. Shaving was a good way to clean your face.

We did have two pairs of undershorts and socks, and most everyone kept a pair of clean socks warm and dry. We had little trouble with men's feet in

North Africa. We only had one uniform. Because the weather was so cold and rainy, it was not practical to take off your clothes to wash them. As a result, a lot of the infantrymen had become infested with lice. In order to eliminate this condition, our company obtained a portable shower and delousing unit from the British, and we operated it for the combat team. The men would be sent in by platoons to take showers. While they were showering, their clothes would go through the delousing unit.

The first delousing unit was constructed using oil-fired, hot-air guns blowing extremely hot air into a tent where the infested uniforms were hung. The hot-air guns were not easy to control, and one time the tent caught fire and all the clothes burned up. This was a major tragedy because no one had two uniforms. There wasn't any way to obtain U.S. Army uniforms because all our supplies came through the British supply system. We could only obtain British uniforms. Many of the infantrymen had mixtures of U.S. and British uniforms. It was a strange-looking group.

Later, we got a delousing unit that operated with steam so we did not burn up any more uniforms. These units sometimes caused the woolen uniforms to shrink and many men had tight fitting uniforms.

The delousing operation could also be dangerous. The men usually had hand grenades attached to their gear. Once, when one man was taking off his clothes, a grenade dropped pulling out the pin. We were lucky that everyone was alert. When the man yelled, "Grenade!" everyone dropped facedown, and the grenade fragments flew over everyone. No one was hurt.

We found that, in the British army, toilet paper was a valuable item. We were issued toilet paper that had "government property" printed on each sheet. We never did obtain very much, and we did not have the luxury of a Sears and Roebuck catalog. Having toilet paper was having wealth. Everyone carried it on his person or nearby in a vehicle. What is wealth? It depends on your environment. To the soldier in North Africa, toilet paper was wealth. So was being clean, or having a dry and warm place to sleep, or getting rid of lice by taking a shower and getting your clothes deloused, or getting clean clothes.

We had one man in our company assigned to cut hair as a part-time job. The haircuts were not stylish, but they made it easier to keep clean.

None of us had been paid for months, but that really did not matter because there wasn't any place to spend the money. There were no leaves or passes. You just stayed on the line. Everyone lost track of time, and I didn't even know what day it was until Father McEvoy (the 18th Infantry chaplain) would hold services. Then I knew it was Sunday. Father McEvoy stayed in our aid station so he could talk to the wounded and record the names of the dead.

I found that you either got used to this life (or at least could put it in the back of your mind) or one of two things would happen. You could go into an extreme nervous state (anxiety state) and have to be sent back to a hospital, or you could take an extreme measure and shoot yourself.

We had a number of men come into the aid station with self-inflicted wounds. Most men shot themselves through the hands and feet. In these cases, the men seemed to be in more pain than the more seriously wounded men. Perhaps it was a feeling of guilt. We had several courts-martial in the aid station, and this corrected the problem.

February 13–16, 1943. Teboursouk, Tunisia

The 18th Infantry was relieved by a British unit, and we turned the shower and delousing unit back to the British and left the area at 1900 hours for Teboursouk. The aid station was set up in a house, and the remainder of the company performed the usual camp duties. There was a French family in the farmhouse, and they let us use one of the rooms for the aid station. The family had a pet dog, and soon after we arrived, the dog ran in front of one of the ambulances and was struck in the head. I could not feel a pulse so I told Pvt. Carney to dispose of the dog. He threw the body over a fence. The next day the dog came wandering over to see us. He seemed all right except that one eye was sticking out about an inch. Not knowing what else to do, I cut it off and placed a bandage on the wound. The one-eyed dog seemed to have fully recovered when we left.

There was also a small unit of Free French soldiers camped nearby, and their sergeant came over to talk to me. The conversation was a mixture of English, French and sign language. However, we seemed to understand each other. He told me they had fresh food and invited me over for a meal. They had just killed a cow or a horse. I wasn't sure which one. They offered me what they considered the choice parts, which were brains and blood pudding. These were not what I considered delicacies. So, rather than insult them, I said I wasn't very hungry but that I would very much like their fresh bread and wine. They either had a good cook or the French people in the house had given them the bread because it was excellent. I hadn't had any fresh bread for months.

The 18th Infantry Combat Team had been in the line at Medjez-el-Bab for 48 days and deserved a rest. However, a heavy German attack was under-way on U.S. forces in the south at Faid Pass, and on February 14, the 18th Infantry Combat Team was ordered to rush south to help stop a breakthrough by the German Afrika Korps at Kasserine.

Six

Kasserine

February 17, 1943. Siliua, Tunisia

The company left Teboursouk at 0130 hours bound for Maktar. We traveled 40 miles by trucks and ambulances and bivouacked near an abandoned farm at Siliua. Siliua was high in the Atlas mountains, and it was very cold. There were a lot of dead cattle in the farmyard. The cattle were frozen solid, and their legs were stiff and sticking straight out. They probably were shot by German planes. We may have been in Africa, but it can get very cold in the mountains of North Africa in the winter. However, when you think of it, we were at about the same latitude as North Carolina, and it can get cold there too.

It was extremely cold that night. Normally, the station platoon would use extra blankets. We carry several hundred to use on the casualties. However, the trucks were all packed, and we did not want to unload the truck. We looked around for the warmest spot out of the wind. The best place we could find was next to a large manure pile. The manure gave off heat as well as sheltering us from the cold wind.

Some of the other men had a better idea. I don't know where they got them, but they put the sheets of a few newspapers between the folds of their blanket and kept very warm. I understand this is an old hobo trick. They probably smelled better than those of us who slept near the manure pile. I often wonder what we smelled like.

February 18, 1943. Maktar, Tunisia

We traveled 37 miles and bivouacked in a farm area south of Maktar at 2000 hours. We arrived in the dark, and it was difficult to see what we were doing. We made minimal use of lights due to German air activity. We had only been there a short time when we heard horrible screams. We had trouble finding the source of the screams. Finally, one man found a three-foot-diameter hole in the ground, and the screams were coming from there.

Someone got a flashlight and looked into the hole. At the bottom of a deep hole, we saw an American soldier screaming. One of the men from the engineer platoon had fallen into the hole and had dropped 15–20 feet straight down. He was completely disoriented and had lost control of himself (with good reason). Finally, we found a rope and pulled him out. He was a nervous wreck and was shaking so bad we had to give him a shot to sedate him. He had fallen into a bell-shaped, earthen underground silo that was used by the Arabs to store grain. Most of the grain had been removed and that accounted for the long fall. There was still some grain on the bottom, which had cushioned his fall so that nothing was broken. He was stunned from the fall and, when he recovered a little, he couldn't see or hear anything and probably thought he had been buried alive. There were more of these empty silos in the vicinity, so we all had to be careful not to fall in them.

The aid station and a few ambulances left the farm and the rest of the company at 1400 hours and moved 21 miles toward the battle area to a location given by map coordinates. The new position was a desolate area full of cactus. We were all apprehensive because it was so exposed. We dug our foxholes and were starting to unload our equipment when a soldier came from behind a knoll and started talking to me in French. I managed to make out he was a sergeant in the Free French Army and was in charge of a battery of 75-mm guns set up behind us. He then pointed to the hills on our left, the hills on our right and finally in front. Each time he said, "Le Boche là!" He was telling us the position we had picked out was in front of the Allied lines and we had better pull out fast. We left hurriedly. Shortly after we left, we discovered Pvt. Morse was missing. Sgt. Pingree and two men with an ambulance went back to hunt for him. They found him in the cactus grove, asleep. He had not heard the order to move out. It was then that we found out that this man, who had been in our company for years, was deaf. He had been able to hide his deafness, and it could have cost him his life. I always thought he was not very smart because when I talked to him he would just smile and not say anything. No one knew he was stone deaf.

Later that day, we set up the aid station in an Arab farmhouse near Sbiba. The farmhouse had been abandoned, and all the livestock and belongings removed. The farm was on a plain at the foot of the coastal mountains at the intersection of two roads. These were not paved but one was the main road to the coast. The area was quite barren and dry. It looked like a desert but without sand. The dirt, if you could call it dirt, was more like fine crushed stone. It did not look very fertile. However, as this was the dry season, maybe with rain it would improve.

The house and barn were built around a small courtyard, where the livestock had been kept. It was a single-story structure with hard-packed earthen floors. The rooms were small, and there was only one closet in the house. The small closet was in the kitchen. There was an engineer's drawing set in the closet so the family must have left hurriedly. The house was not far from the mountain pass where the Germans were expected to try to break through on their way to Tebessa, where the large Allied supply dump was located. This was a very exposed position, which caused us some concern. We would try to keep most of our traffic with the ambulances to after dark, so that we would not draw attention to our position.

The remainder of the company, including the kitchen truck, had bivouacked in a dry river bed 10½ miles to the rear. Our meals were brought to us at night.

February 19–28, 1943. Sbiba, Tunisia

The 18th Infantry had taken up positions to cover the small town of Sbiba, which was located at the mountain pass the Germans would use to come through the coastal mountain range to the interior of Tunisia. All flanking positions had been sown with mines, and it would be very dangerous for anyone to get off the road. The combat team was now attached to the U.S. 34th Division. We were evacuating casualties to the clearing company of the 109th Medical Battalion of the 34th Division.

On February 19, the 18th Infantry Combat Team repulsed a German probing attack and inflicted heavy losses on the enemy. During this battle, we had a lot of casualties and for the next few days were kept busy. Not only did we have members of the 18th Infantry Combat Team as casualties, but quite

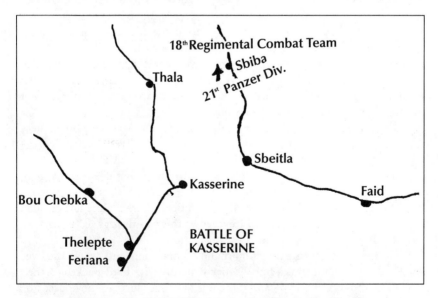

Position of the 18th RCT in the battle of Kasserine, Tunisia.

a few wounded German soldiers went through our aid station. These Germans were all members of the German Afrika Korps commanded by General Rommel. Some of the German soldiers had fought in Russia. I talked to one who had a red star that he got from a Russian soldier. He gave me the star, which I still have. For a while, I wore it on my cap until I found that some wounded men thought I was a general. I did not wear it after that. I also collected other German souvenirs and sent them home.

Some of the wounded died in our aid station. Because we had no place to put the bodies, we had to bury the dead. We wrapped each body in a blanket and dug graves near the outside wall of the house. We thought digging the graves would be easy because we expected to hit sand. We were wrong. The soil was very hard, and we had to use picks. We dug the first grave about six feet deep. The others were not as deep. On each grave, we put up a cross made from the limbs of scrub trees growing nearby. We then nailed one of each man's identification tags (dog tags) on his cross. Eventually there were three American soldiers and two Germans buried there.

Father McEvoy, the combat team chaplain, was staying at the aid station, and he held short burial ceremonies. He also took the information to pass on to the graves registration people. Perhaps the chaplain's most difficult job was to collect the dead men's meager personal belongings and send them back to their families. Father McEvoy had been the 18th Infantry chaplain for many years and knew most of the men in the 18th. He had been very shaken by the loss of 350 men in our last action about six weeks ago. It must be hard to write letters to the soldiers' families and enclose the few possessions the men had.

I often wonder if anyone ever recovered the bodies. It was a desolate place and, after the battle was over, there would be no reason for anyone to go near this house except the owner.

Father McEvoy was also concerned about the wounded men and would talk to them before we would send them back to the clearing company. One time, our company commander, who was a doctor, told us that an American soldier had died, and his body was put aside to be buried. Father McEvoy went to the body to record his name and collect his belongings and found the soldier was still alive. We brought the man back in the aid station and gave him blood plasma. We then sent him back to the clearing company.

The Arab owner of the farm came down from the mountains several times while we were there. He was taking a big risk because he had to cross a minefield. He was either very lucky or his camel was not heavy enough to set the mines off. He rode his camel, or dromedary. It had one hump. The camel was a nasty animal, and every time I would go near it, it would snarl, bare its yellow, stained teeth and spit at me. The owner offered to let me ride it but I declined because I thought it would bite me.

The Arab seemed to be an educated man, and we talked. He could speak French, and I could speak a little French. He must have taken pity on me because the second time he came, he brought a small French-English dictionary and gave it to me. He said another American soldier had given it to him before the beginning of the German breakthrough at Kasserine. I repaid him (perhaps) by giving him some C rations. He said another soldier had given him some C rations, but they were not as good as cous-cous. If we were still there the next time he came, he would bring some cous-cous. I found out later that cous-cous is a grain used by the Arabs to make soup or gruel. I once tried some in Marseille but, to me, it was no great delicacy.

March 1–9, 1943. Sbiba, Tunisia

The aid station was operating as usual. We had several wounded Germans in the aid station when a U.S. counterintelligence officer came in to question them. If the officer had not been in a U.S. uniform, I would have thought he was a German officer.

He talked to the German prisoners in German and almost immediately had the walking wounded men standing at attention. The men answered all his questions.

We also had a war correspondent go through the station. He was not hurt bad but was evacuated. He did leave his typewriter and that had to be sent back later.

Our area was strafed by German planes on March 3 and March 4. As a result, Battery B, 431st CAA, had two anti-aircraft guns set up in the area for protection. This particular unit had just arrived from Algiers. They had a new radar setup to help them direct their guns. Soon after they set up, one of their jeeps drove up to the aid station. An officer was sitting in the jeep holding a Bouncing Betty mine in his lap. This is a German anti-personnel mine that looks like a five-inch-diameter cannonball. It has a stem sticking up about two feet, and on this stem are three six-inch prongs. If anything hits one of these prongs, it will explode. The Germans normally bury these in the ground with the three prong detonator exposed. When anyone hits a prong, the mine jumps three or four feet in the air and explodes. They are quite deadly. The officer asked, "What is it? We found it near our battery." I told him, "It is a mine. Be very careful with it and get away from us. Take it to the engineers and have them detonate it. If you want to set it off yourself set it down easily and shoot at it from a distance."

He must have been successful because he did not pass through our aid station as a casualty.

March 10, 1943. Sbiba, Tunisia

The Germans had withdrawn and the threat was over, so we closed the aid station and the company moved to Rohia. We then proceeded eight miles

west and bivouacked in a field to wait for the rest of the combat team to move
out toward Tébessa, Algeria. We left the field at 1700 hours.

March 11, 1943. Bou Chebka, Tunisia

It was a long, dark drive. At one time during the drive, we were following in the long convoy of vehicles when the road became very rough and
bumpy. The Germans still had control of the air so we did not use headlights
in night convoys. We just followed the truck in front of us. After a while, the
convoy stopped and, after some delay, turned in a different direction and eventually the road became normal. Because the night was so dark the lead vehicle had been following a line of telephone poles on the side of the road. The
poles had left the side of the road and had gone across a field. The lead driver had just kept following the poles. We arrived at Bou Chebka at 0830
hours after driving all night. We were now far away from any combat area,
and we bivouacked while waiting for orders.

Seven

El Guettar

March 12–14, 1943. Bou Chebka, Tunisia

This was a staging area to prepare for the next operation. We were told that we would be here a while so we proceeded to check our vehicles, supplies and equipment. Now, for the first time in three months, we were in the U.S. Army supply system and were able to obtain U.S. Army equipment and food. We used to think U.S. Army rations were not very good but they are better than the British rations. Except for the rum ration!

We had a chance to relax and rest for a few days. We took showers and changed our clothes after the shower. We did this by picking out the proper size or as close as possible from the pile of washed uniforms available at the shower area. A few of the men had washed their woolen uniforms in hot water. The clothes had shrunk so much that they could hardly get them on. Now, they could pick out a better size from the pile. The men who had mixed British and American uniforms could now discard the British uniforms.

The entire 1st Infantry Division was assembling in this location. This was the first time, in Tunisia, the division had been together under the division commanding general. Most units of the 1st Infantry Division had been fighting in Tunisia for months. Some had even been airlifted from Oran, Algeria, in November 1942. The British 1st Army was in control of the Tunisian campaign, and they had committed the 1st Division piecemeal to block or counter German moves.

March 15, 1943. Feriana, Tunisia

The company left Bou Chebka at 2400 hours (midnight) and went by motor convoy to Feriana. This was an all-night drive and, because of the blackout, it was a hair-raising ride. Most of the drivers were tired and not very alert, and the convoy was going quite fast. During the trip, the driver of the ambulance I was in fell asleep, and the ambulance went off the road and hit a tree. The damage was not severe but a few of the men in the back of the ambulance were thrown out of their seats and suffered cuts and bruises. We bivouacked at Feriana.

March 16, 1943. Gafsa

The combat team left Feriana and moved to a position five miles north of Gafsa. This was the assembly point in preparation for an attack on Gafsa.

March 17–21, 1943. Gafsa (3 miles southeast), Tunisia

The entire 1st Infantry Division was to attack Gafsa. The attack was preceded by a bombing strike on the town. We watched as 12 U.S. medium bombers came over and dropped their load of bombs. I did not see any enemy anti-aircraft fire. After the bombers had finished, the infantry went into Gafsa and found that the town, which had been held by the Italians, had been abandoned.

Gafsa was a former French Foreign Legion garrison, and it looked like a Hollywood set from *Beau Geste*. There was a large fort, which probably could have been of some use to fight off Arab camel troops armed only with rifles, but it would not have been much of a defense against modern weapons. This is probably why the Italians abandoned Gafsa. Gafsa is at the border of the Sahara desert, and the soil was like beach sand. We now felt that we were in a real desert. The aid station was set up a few miles from Gafsa, and we were evacuating to the clearing company of the 1st Medical Battalion. There were no casualties from the 18th Infantry, but we did take care of the casualties from our bombing raid on Gafsa. They were all Arab civilians.

I asked one of the French authorities in Gafsa if any of the French people had been hurt. His answer was, "There were no real casualties. Only a few Arabs were killed and wounded and we lost some cattle and dogs."

I am sure that this was the attitude that caused the Algerians to eventually rebel against French rule and throw the French out of North Africa.

Recently, I was asked if it bothered me to see that civilians were killed and wounded as a result of the battles. I had to think about that question. At first, it did bother me very much but, as I saw more wounded and dead, I guess I came to regard civilian casualties as a fact of life, a natural event, and it bothered me less. However, we did not see many civilian casualties because our battles were usually in areas where the civilians had fled. I did feel very bad about the civilian casualties in the landing at Normandy because they were the first civilian casualties who could be considered allies.

We were able to go into Gafsa and into the fort. I even got to swim in the pool in the fort.

We were now in the U.S. II Army Corps along with the 9th and 34th Infantry Divisions and the 1st Armored Division. Gen. George S. Patton was the new II Corps commander, and he made sure we all knew it. We still had woolen uniforms, and it was hot in the desert. Now, Patton insisted we had to wear leggings, full helmets and ties all the time. Any soldier who disobeyed his dress order would be fined $25. I guess Patton thought money meant something to us. We all had some money but it was sort of valueless because we did not have any place to spend it. Many of us were having most of our pay sent home, and the little we did get would accumulate or would be lost gambling. The division must not have enforced the order because I never did hear of anyone paying a fine.

The aid station was now set up on the road to El Guettar between Gafsa and El Guettar. Along this road, there was a large oasis called Garden of Allah. The oasis had a large pool of water fed by a spring, and there were many large palm trees growing on the terrace around the pool. I was able to visit the oasis for a short time, and while I was there, a small Arab boy came up and wanted to sell me some dates. Of course, I thought they would be from the local palm trees. When I looked at the package, I noticed the printing "Packed in the U.S.A." It probably came from the U.S. Army supplies abandoned when Rommel's Afrika Korps broke through our lines some weeks ago. The enterprising boy had picked up some supplies and was in business.

We were still under occasional air attacks and had to keep digging fox-holes everywhere we went. There must have been millions of foxholes all over Tunisia. The digging around Gafsa was excellent. The ground was sandy, and you could dig with abandon. It was not like the rocky areas in the mountains where the digging was hard and many times we would hit rocks and shale.

Sgt. Ken Woods found the digging so good he decided to make the ideal foxhole. He dug one about two feet in diameter and perhaps six feet deep. In this hole, he would have to get a direct hit from a shell or bomb to be hurt. It would be almost impossible to get hit from a strafing plane. He had no sooner finished the hole when a German plane came over and strafed the area. We all dived into our holes. After the plane left, we could hear some muffled shouting. It was Sgt. Woods, crying for help. All we could see of him was his two shoes sticking out of his foxhole. He had dived into the hole head first and couldn't get out. The foxhole was so narrow that his arms were pinned, and we had to pull him out. Even in the perfect foxhole you have to be careful.

The 1st Reconnaissance Troop of the 1st Infantry Division was now chasing the Italians retreating toward El Guettar. El Guettar was on the road that led to Gabès, a port on the coast of Tunisia. If this port could be taken, the coastal road heading north would be cut. Rommel's Afrika Korps, which was being pushed north from Libya into Tunisia by the British 8th Army, could be kept from joining the German army near Tunis and would be surrounded. The road to Gabès went through the coastal mountain range at El Guettar and was defended by Italian army units under General Rommel. The terrain was rugged, and there were steep rock cliffs on both sides of the road. It was ideal for defense.

El Guettar was attacked on March 21 by units of the 1st Infantry Division. The town and surrounding areas were soon taken, along with 700 prisoners (mostly Italians).

March 22–23, 1943. El Guettar, Tunisia

The 18th Infantry Combat Team moved into the El Guettar area on the 22d. We were now in the coastal mountains and advancing on a dirt road through a mountain pass. The Germans were very sensitive to this move and sent over a lot of aircraft to harass us. At one point, we had to pull our vehicles off the road into a field so we could disperse the vehicles. We were there with 30–40 other trucks, ambulances and halftracks, waiting for word to move, when a flight of low-flying, twin-engine German bombers (JU-88s) came over and dropped their bombs among the vehicles. Most of the soldiers dropped into their slit trenches, but some of the men stayed upright and shot back. As a result, we had quite a few casualties. We had to pick up the wounded and dead.

I took an ambulance and a litter squad and went to where I heard a shout for "Medics." The first casualty was a man who had been standing in an armored halftrack shooting a 50-caliber machine gun at the attacking planes. A bomb landed on the ground about 20 feet from him, and one of the steel fragments angled upward and took off the top of his head. He was dead so we took the body out of the halftrack and left it on the ground to be picked up later. Other men who were closer to the exploding bomb were not touched because they were lying down, and the bomb fragments went over their heads. If the man had kept his head below the armored side of the halftrack while he was firing, he wouldn't have been killed.

Another man was hit in the arm and shoulder. He was bleeding quite badly. I cut off his shirt around the wound with my bandage shears, poured in sulfa powder and applied the large dressing. I was writing up the tag on the man when another flight of German bombers came over. I laid down beside the wounded man and watched the bombers. They came over very low and, when one was directly over me, I saw the bombs release. However, the bombs kept going forward so they missed us.

The German planes were not using anti-personnel bombs in these raids. They dropped 100-pound bombs that made holes two to three feet in diameter in the hard-packed surface. During both bombing runs, all of the halftracks

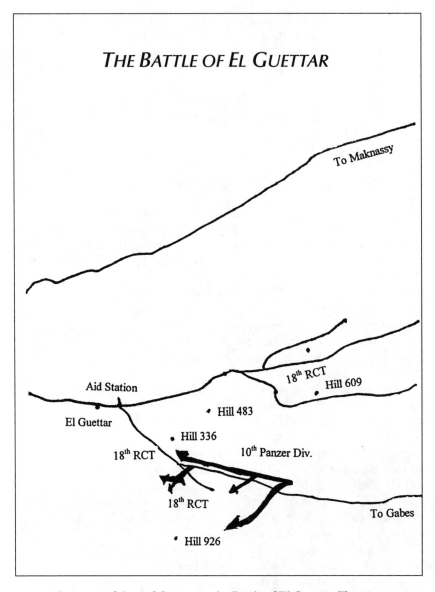

Location of the Aid Station in the Battle of El Guettar, Tunisia.

and the infantry were shooting everything they had at the planes. The sky was full of red tracers, but none of the German planes were hit.

This second bombing run did no damage so we quickly collected all the wounded men and sent them back to the clearing company. We then got back on the road and drove until we came to where the road divided. We set up the aid station at the road junction. Here, we could receive casualties from the two battalions that were attacking along the bare brown mountains on both sides of the pass.

On March 23 at 0600 hours, the 18th Infantry Combat Team came under heavy attack from the German 10th Panzer Division. This was the German division that had led the breakthrough in the battle of France in 1940. With the 10th Panzer was the Italian Centauro Division, the German Ramcke Brigade and part of the 21st Panzer Division.

The 18th Infantry Combat Team had two field artillery battalions and the 601st Tank Destroyer Battalion to help fight off the German tanks. The 601st was equipped with halftracks that had 75-mm guns mounted on them. They were no match for the German tanks, which had 88-mm high-velocity guns. The 601st put up a good fight. In doing so, all the tank destroyers of Companies B and C of the 601st were destroyed.

The German attack split the infantry from the artillery. Some of the artillery pieces had to be temporarily abandoned because the German tanks had overrun their position. The 18th Infantry Combat Team continued its fierce resistance and inflicted so much damage on the Germans that they stopped their attack at 0900 hours.

The Germans resumed the attack at 1700 hours. This time they had infantry leading the tanks. The 18th Infantry Combat Team was fighting to maintain its strong defensive position with help from a tank destroyer unit, which had just arrived in the area a few hours earlier. This unit was equipped with a new type of tank destroyer, that had a three-inch naval gun mounted on a full-tracked, heavily armored vehicle. It was the first time this type of tank destroyer had ever been in action.

The furious artillery barrages and the heavy mortar fire from the infantry destroyed many German tanks. The 10th Panzer Division was unable to break through our lines, and after suffering large losses, withdrew to defensive positions.

The cost on both sides was heavy. The Germans lost 35–40 tanks and many men. We got some of their wounded in our aid station. We lost 20 of the 28 small tank destroyers (M-3) and 7 of the 10 new tank destroyers (M-10).

During this battle, our aid station was set up along the only road that was used by all the troops in the 18th Infantry Combat Team as well as by the other units engaged in this battle. We saw the company of the 899th Tank Destroyer Battalion, the one with the 3-inch naval guns, go by the aid station. They had much bigger guns than our old tank destroyers. I thought they could really do a job on the German tanks. However, in a short time, we started to get battle casualties from this unit. While they helped in turning back the German attack, they lost quite a few men.

The battered hulks of seven of the new M-10 tank destroyers were retrieved the next day and were left in a field near our aid station. I looked them over and saw where the German 88-mm shells punched holes clean through the 3-inch armor plate and then exploded inside the tank destroyer. Some shells even went out the other side. These tank destroyers were not like tanks because the turrets were open at the top. This made it easier for men to get out if the tank destroyer was hit and started to burn.

During this battle, the Germans had control of the air and strafed and bombed often. The German planes not only came over and bombed and strafed during the day, but they would come over many times at night. They would drop flares on little parachutes. When they identified a possible target, they would drop canisters full of small bombs. These canisters would open up in the air and spread the bombs over a large area.

Because our aid station was out in the open, we made our slit trenches deep and covered them. You could not have a peaceful sleep unless you had a covered hole. Sleeping in a small, covered foxhole is not pleasant because the dirt keeps trickling down on you and your blanket. Everything gets dirty and the air is not good. You wonder. *What if a bomb lands nearby? Will the hole collapse and smother me?* This did happen to some men in the 5th Field Artillery.

One night, I was sleeping in the foxhole when I felt something moving on me. At first I thought it was a snake, and I crawled out fast. Later, I came to the conclusion that it was a mole because I saw the hole where it had come into my slit trench.

We were working steadily day and night during this heavy attack. Because our location was on the only road that was close to the main action, we not only evacuated casualties from the 18th Infantry but from 22 other units, as well as German wounded. The Germans in the Afrika Korps were dressed differently than the Germans we had encountered in northern Tunisia and seemed to be better disciplined. Most of them were blond with blue eyes. We had heard that Rommel had an elite force in North Africa.

We erected a tent so we could work at night with lights. In the tent we had two setups where simple operations could be performed. During heavy periods of action, which would be in daylight, we had a space problem. We had so many wounded that we had to put them in the field near the tent. During the day, only the wounded that could be helped by some type of an operation, such as sewing up a deep chest wound or tying off an artery, would go into the tent. At one time, we had 40 or 50 wounded men at our aid station with more coming in all the time. Even with all 12 ambulances taking the wounded to the clearing company, the number kept building. We also had a problem with some of the doctors because they would spend so much time with the worst cases (who could not live). We had to select the ones to be worked on. It was bedlam.

One young soldier had been severely shot in both his legs by a strafing German plane. He was crying, "My father lost both of his legs in World War I and now I am going to lose my legs."

All we could do for him was to stop the bleeding, put sulfa and dress-ings on his wounds, give him a shot of morphine and send him back to the clearing company. Later, one of our doctors told me he thought the man would lose his legs.

After one of the long periods of action, when things had quieted down, we needed something to revive us. We wanted a hot drink, and our kitchen truck was not with us. I remembered one of the medical chests contained a can of powdered malt drink mix. It had to be mixed with hot water. How-ever, we had no container to heat the water except an enamel pail. The pail contained all the bloody dressings and bloody clothes we took off the wounded men. So, we washed out the pail and used it to heat up the drink. We also found out that a collecting aid station is not an optimistic place to gauge the progress of a battle. We would get our news from wounded men, who felt we were losing the battle. Combine this with the utter exhaustion of working 36 hours without any sleep, and we were sure the battle was lost. We did doze off a few minutes at a time. After a few days, some of our men would start to hallucinate. We then made each man go to his hole and sleep until he had at least eight hours' sleep.

As usual, we had to take care of the dead bodies. Some, who had been killed in the tank destroyers, were hard to remove. One gunner in a small tank destroyer had been killed as he was loading a long anti-tank shell. He was wedged in under the breech, and it was difficult to remove the body. When I was recording his name, I noticed he was from Lawrence, Massachusetts. His name was Quellette. I lived in greater Lawrence, and I remembered a Quel-lette who played football for Lawrence High School. I often wondered if it was the same man. I thought I should inform his parents and give them the details of his death. But years passed before the war was over and I finally got back to the States. Then, I did not see any point in reopening old sad mem-ories.

K Company of the 18th Infantry received a presidential citation for its stand at El Guettar. The citation reads, "K Company against tank and infantry attacks, despite heavy losses, repulsed savage thrusts and held a strategic posi-tion. If lost it would have impaired future operations."

March 24, 1943. El Guettar, Tunisia

We had men in our own company wounded. Pfc. Chester A. Piasczyk was seriously wounded (laceration, left eye; shell fragments in abdomen, left arm and hand) while driving his ambulance through a mine field near Gafsa. Pfc. John J. Maloney was slightly wounded while driving an ambulance through a minefield near Gafsa. Both were evacuated to the clearing company of the 1st Medical Battalion.

March 25–26, 1943. El Guettar, Tunisia

The aid station was operating and evacuation was proceeding under heavy artillery fire and strafing by German planes. The Gabès-Gafsa road was being attacked quite often by German Stuka dive bombers, ME-109 fighter bombers, Fockewolf-190 fighter bombers and JU-88 bombers.

When the planes came over, we would all dive into the nearest foxhole. One time, three men tried to pile in one hole, and there was not enough room. Pvt. Jim Carney yelled out, "Ho, ho. No more room." He was kidded about this for several years.

Jim was a very valuable man. He was a big man and older than most of us. Before he was drafted, he had worked as an attendant in a mental hospital in up state New York. He was the one who could restrain men with anxiety state when they became violent.

We had our aid station set up in a tent that had a red cross on it, but it must not have been very visible to the German pilots. I don't think they would have bombed our area if they had known it was an aid station.

March 27, 1943. El Guettar, Tunisia

The aid station was operating under heavy fire, and the 18th Infantry needed more help in carrying wounded men out of the mountains, so a corporal and ten litter bearers were sent to the 2d Battalion, 18th Infantry to help in evacuating wounded.

Another man in our company was wounded. Pvt. Russell H. Taylor had a compound fracture of his right ankle just above his foot, and it was almost severed. The enemy artillery shell fragments also hit his left hand. We evacuated him to the 51st Medical Battalion.

The night attacks by the German planes continued, and we got to expect it. About every two hours, we would hear the throbbing engines of the JU-88 and they would drop their large load of small anti-personnel bombs. They did not do much damage, but they did keep us awake. When we heard the bombs whistling down, we never were sure where they might land and so everyone started to shiver a little. The nights did get cold there and the combination of cold and fright made everyone get up after the plane left and relieve his kidneys.

March 28–31, 1943. El Guettar, Tunisia

The aid station and evacuation were operating as usual. We had a visit from the division commander, General Allen, who was looking over the situation. He asked how things were going, and we complained about the German air activity and our lack of anti-aircraft and fighter plane protection.

Finally, as the battle was about over, the British sent over a flight of Spitfires that intercepted a flight of 12 of the slow German Stuka dive bombers. In a few minutes, they shot all of them down, and everyone was cheering. One of the German pilots was able to parachute out and he came down, over the 18th Infantry position. Someone decided to get revenge and started shooting at the pilot. Soon, the sky was full of red tracers. I saw the pilot slump in the parachute and I suppose he was killed.

Maybe General Allen used his influence to get the British fighter planes over to give us all a little relief.

April 1–8, 1943. El Guettar, Tunisia

The aid station and evacuation were operating as usual. With litter bearers and ambulances from the 18th Infantry, we went to the clearing company of the 1st Medical Battalion and the 48th Evacuation Hospital.

April 9, 1943. Sabet, Tunisia

We moved from El Guettar to a position southwest of Sabet and set up the aid station. However, there was little activity. We heard that the Germans had withdrawn to positions farther back. We all felt good about the action at El Guettar because here the U.S. Army had won its first victory over the German army.

We later found out that the performance of the 1st Division in this battle so impressed the commander of the German Afrika Korps, General Rommel, that he noted in his diary, "The Americans learned in one battle what the British had not learned in two years. After their defeat at Kasserine, the Americans came back in a few months and even using their obsolete weapons, with no air support, was able to defeat a superior German force."*

Our company was cited in division orders for the excellent work we performed at El Guettar in the support of 22 U.S. Army units.

April 10–13, 1943. Gafsa, Tunisia

We moved 26 miles from Sabet to Gafsa by vehicles. We cleaned up and prepared for the next battle.

*Quoted in Brendan Phibbs' The Other Side of Time (Boston: Little, Brown, 1987), page 243.

Eight

Victory in North Africa

April 14–17, 1943. Bou Kadra
(5½ miles northeast), Tunisia

We left Gafsa and traveled north by truck 145 miles to Bou Kadra and bivouacked. Here we were able to rest and clean up. The ride was not pleasant because we were in a long convoy of vehicles and had to go up and down some steep mountains. The twisting roads and the high speed caused a lot of men to become sick. It was motion sickness similar to seasickness. Or, perhaps, the upset stomachs were caused by the Spam sandwiches we had to eat on the move. Even now, I can't tolerate Spam.

This move was a tremendous logistical switch. The entire U.S. II Army Corps had to move to the north flank of the British 1st Army units, which were facing Tunis and Bizerte, and cross their supply and communication lines. This put the 18th Infantry Combat Team in an area near where it had been fighting last winter. This time, we were north of Medjez-el-Bab and were on the road to Mateur. Mateur is about 20 miles southeast of the port of Bizerte and northeast of Tunis. This had been the scene of the delaying action by the Germans in the race for Tunis the previous fall and winter. The Allied forces had almost won the race. The 18th Infantry Combat Team's battle of Longstop Hill last Christmas had been to help stabilize the line until the attack on Tunis and Bizerte could be resumed.

The attack was now to be resumed, and the British 1st Army was to retake Longstop Hill in this offensive. We in the U.S. II Army Corps were to attack towards Mateur and Bizerte. The area looked a lot different than it had four months ago and very different than the stark mountains and desert around El Guettar. Here, back in the Atlas mountains, there were green valleys and large fields of scarlet poppies.

The Germans and Italians were now corraled in the northeast corner of Tunisia. They were in the area bounded by Mateur, Bizerte, Tunis and Cape Bon. The British 8th Army was pushing up from the south, and the British 1st Army was attacking from the west. The U.S. II Army Corps was to attack east in a line from the British 1st Army north to the Mediterranean.

April 18, 1943. Roum-es-Souk
(4 miles west) Tunisia

Our company left Bou Kadra and bivouacked 4 miles west of Roum-es-Souk. This was a temporary stop so the 18th Infantry Combat Team could get into position for the forthcoming attack.

April 19–25, 1943. Oued Zarga, Tunisia

We left Roum-es-Souk and traveled by truck to Oued Zarga. We arrived at 1400 hours and set up the aid station in preparation to receive casualties.

The German forces facing the 1st Infantry Division consisted of the German 334th Infantry Division, the crack Barenthin Engineer Regiment of the Luftwaffe and parts of the 10th Panzer Division. The terrain was mountainous, and the enemy was strongly entrenched on the commanding ground. This was a battle for the highest mountain tops because whoever held the best observation post could direct artillery fire into the other lines. The enemy positions were well-prepared and well-camouflaged.

The attack at Mateur was launched over broken rocky hills that tore shoes and clothing. The infantry had to carry the heavy mortars, machine guns and ammunition up and down these mountains. At the same time, they were trying to dodge enemy shell fire and small arms fire. All approaches were well-protected with German land mines. In an attack on just one hill, the engineers cleared 1,800 mines from the area.

In a night attack, the 18th Infantry Combat Team made early advances but was later pushed from the high ground by the 10th Panzer Division counterattacks. Finally, after a stiff fight, the 18th regained the high ground. All of this resulted in many casualties, and we were kept busy both day and night.

We had to set up a large tent so we could work during the night. It was difficult because the German planes were very active and were dropping their canisters of anti-personnel bombs all over our area at night. We received many casualties, and our aid station was soon filled with wounded men. While there were many wounds from shell fire and small arms, we now saw bayonet and knife wounds. This meant hand-to-hand fighting was going on. After some hours, the flow of wounded slowed down because the hill had been secured.

However, the German air force knew the vital hill was in our hands, and they proceeded to bomb the area. While night bombing is not as effective as daylight bombing, it is nerve-wracking. Because the aid station was situated at a strategic crossroad, we got our share of the activity. The German bombers would come over and after releasing parachute flares to light up the targets, would drop their canisters of anti-personnel bombs. These

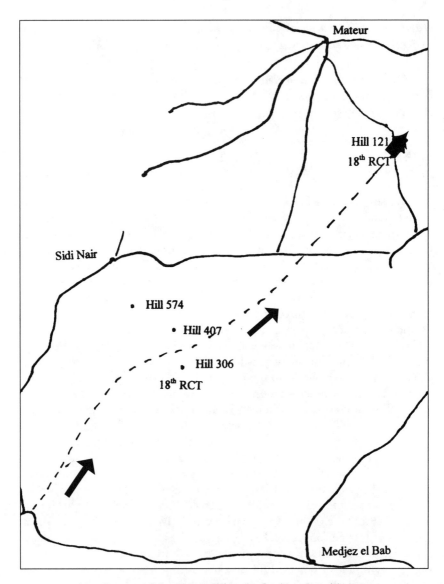

Attack route of the 18th RCT in the final battle in Tunisia.

canisters would open above the target and scatter scores of small bombs over a large area.

Late one night, we had a wounded soldier on the operating litter with a deep shell-fragment wound in his chest. It had penetrated his lung, and it was so bad he was breathing through the wound and was expelling frothy blood from both the open wound and his mouth. The doctor, Capt. Tegmeyer, and

I were starting to close the wound with sutures when several German planes came over and dropped flares over our position. Everyone left the tent and dived into their holes, and I was left alone with the wounded man. I couldn't leave a badly wounded man who needed immediate treatment alone during a bombing raid, so I finished the suturing, put on sulfa powder and a dressing and then sealed the wound with strips of wide adhesive tape. This made it possible for the man to breathe more normally, and he felt much better. When the bombing stopped, we sent the man directly to the 15th Evacuation Hospital rather than the clearing company.

The battle was continuing, and we were evacuating so many casualties that we were all exhausted. This resulted in one of our own men breaking down. We had to evacuate him to the 15th Evacuation Hospital with anxiety state.

The original battle strategy was to have the U.S. II Corps draw off the German strength and not advance. But the American high command wanted to prove that four American divisions could fight as well together as the more experienced British 8th Army. So we were ordered to advance over almost impossible terrain.

The 18th Infantry was awarded a presidential citation for its part in this battle.

The citation reads:

On April 23, 1943, the 2nd Battalion of the 18th Infantry fought the battle of hill 350, which opened the way for the U.S. 1st Armored Division to roll across the plains of Mateur. It was a desperate battle featured by the use of bayonets and close in fighting until the determined defenders were driven from the hill. A powerful enemy counterattack pushed the battalion from their newly won position, but the rifle companies came right back to again defeat the Nazi forces. This time, despite their weakened condition, they firmly held their hard won victory.

Ernie Pyle wrote of this battle:

It was a war of such intensity as Americans on this side of the ocean had not known before. It was a battle without letup. It was a war of drenching artillery and hidden mines, and walls of machine gun fire and even of the barbaric bayonet. It was an exhausting, cruel, last-ditch kind of war and those who went through it would seriously doubt that war could be any worse.*

April 26–May 1, 1943. Mateur
(15 miles south), Tunisia

We moved from Oued Zarga to a point 15 miles south of Mateur. The aid station was set up, and evacuations continued. We were now beginning to receive many wounded German soldiers.

*In the booklet The First published by The Stars and Stripes (ETO, 1945), page 16.

Another hill was then pounded by artillery to prepare it for the next day's attack. The artillery bombardment resumed the next morning prior to the infantry attack. However, there were signs that the Germans were preparing to withdraw and, later that day, instead of attacking the hill, the infantry bypassed it and went on to take the vital hill on the left flank of the Tine valley. Because the combat team was way out in front of an adjoining division, we had to stop and wait for the units of the 34th Division to come abreast of us. We now had it easy for a couple of days.

The following day, we got word that there were some wounded and dead Germans on the hill that had been bypassed. I took several ambulances and a group of litter bearers up a long dirt road to the top of one of the high hills. We parked near an old Arab hut and sent the litter bearers out to look for casualties. I went into the hut and found a large German soldier on a litter. He was dead and must have been dead for several days because the sickish sweet odor of death was strong. I had just told some of the men to load the body into the ambulance when one man shouted, "We have a live one here!"

I went over to a small bush, and lying under the bush, was a German soldier with a bad leg wound. What was most unusual was the mass of maggots on the open wound. I examined the wound carefully, and it was the cleanest wound I had ever seen. The wounded man interrupted my inspection by pleading, "Vasser. Vasser."

I gave him my canteen, and he took a long drink. I let him keep it for a while, as I studied his leg some more. The leg had a long wide gash below the knee and was open to the bones, but the bones did not seem to be broken. The man had lost so much blood he was very weak. I did not touch the wound because I wanted the doctors to see the maggots. We carefully put him on the litter, and the litter bearers carried him over near the shack.

In the meantime, other litter bearers had found another wounded German. He was in very poor shape. His whole body was puffed up, and he was barely conscious and was scratching himself all the time. He had a wound in his abdomen and, while it had stopped bleeding, it appeared to me that he had some serious internal injury. He also wanted water but, because of his abdominal injury, all we would do was wet his lips. We could not find any more wounded or dead in this place so we loaded the two wounded soldiers and the dead one into an ambulance and went back to the aid station.

While the doctors were examining the two wounded men, I asked about the maggots. One of the doctors said, "The man was very lucky. The maggots probably saved his life. Years ago maggots, were used as a way to save people with gangrene. The maggots ate all the dead and decaying flesh and cleaned it up."

There wasn't much we could do so I cleaned all the maggots out of the leg and packed the clean wound with sulfa powder and dressed the wound. We gave the German a bottle of blood plasma and a shot of morphine.

The other German was not as fortunate. His wound was very serious, and the doctor thought he would not recover as he was in the last stages of uremia. We cleaned the wound and sprinkled it with sulfa and applied a dressing. We did not give him any plasma because it probably would increase his discomfort. Both of the Germans were sent back to the clearing company.

During this battle, our ambulance drivers had a difficult time because of the bad roads, the rough terrain and the constant shelling. The ambulances were full of holes from shell fragments and mine fragments. Several had even been hit by small arms fire. One time, when we were putting a litter in an ambulance, we had trouble getting it in because we found the driver was now carrying a demijohn of wine. He would periodically take a drink. His assistant driver told us that he would even take a drink in his sleep. However, he was an excellent man and not only managed to do his job well but he was able to keep the demijohn full.

May 2, 1943. Mateur (15 miles south), Tunisia

The aid station was still operating and, on May 3, Mateur was captured. Again, we were given the job of collecting and identifying the dead. This was a big job because there were many casualties, and the mountainous terrain made it difficult to pick up the bodies. The odor of the dead permeated everything because some bodies had been out in the hot sun for several days. We started by using the ambulances to carry the dead back to the collection point, where we recorded their names and units. The smell the bodies left in the ambulances was so bad that we thought it could adversely affect the wounded men so we started to use trucks. Because there were so many dead, we had to use 2½–ton trucks. We would bring the trucks as close as possible to the battle sites and carry the bodies on litters over the mountainous terrain to the trucks.

The bodies had been lying out in the hot African sun for two to three days, and we had to take the bodies down the steep mountains and load them on the trucks. The bodies had started to decompose, and the sickish sweet odor of death permeated everything. Some bodies were rigid from rigor mortis but most of them were now limp and were not in good shape and were hard to handle. I will never forget the time we had unloading the trucks full of bodies. What a horrible sight it is to see a 2½–ton truck full of dead American soldiers. We laid all the bodies out and tried to identify them. One time, we only had the man's head and were not sure what body it belonged to. There were some bodies that did not have dog tags so we could not identify the soldiers. We put the bodies in mattress covers and sent them back to a collection point. I hoped we'd never have to do this again.

Years later, I was living in the Schenectady, New York, area, where there was an Army depot. They were receiving the disinterred bodies of soldiers killed in World War II as requested by their families. I wonder if the families knew that it was very possible that the body they buried was not the one they thought it was. In my opinion, the bodies were best left in the cemeteries near the battlefields.

May 3, 1943. Mateur (12 miles South), Tunisia

We moved the aid station forward. Evacuation was proceeding normally, and the battle was less intense.

May 4–12, 1943. Munchar, Tunisia

We set up the aid station. However, as we had been squeezed out by other advancing units, we were not having any more battle casualties.

We were near Mateur and were able to see a little of the area. It was here that I had my first pizza. There were quite a few Italians in this part of Tunisia, and they had introduced the pizza. It was not like the pizza we now know in the U.S. It was made with bread, sliced tomato and mozzarella cheese.

The Germans surrendered on May 12, 1943, and the fighting in North Africa ended. In this 17-day battle, the 1st Division had 103 men killed, 1,245 wounded and 682 missing. The Allied forces took 267,000 enemy prisoners in northern Tunisia.

May 13, 1943. Guelma, Algeria

We left Munchar for Guelma by vehicle and bivouacked on the outskirts of the town.

May 14, 1943. Bene Manseur, Algeria

We left Guelma for Bene Manseur and bivouacked for the night. We now knew that we were going back to Algeria to prepare for the next operation. Whatever that might be.

May 15, 1943. L'Arba, Algeria

We left Bene Manseur for L'Arba by vehicle and arrived at 1700 hours after traveling 125 miles. We bivouacked for the night.

L'Arba is a suburb of Algiers, and some of us were given passes to Algiers, the capital of Algeria. It is a large city, a seaport, and is situated on the seaward slope of high hills, overlooking a large semi-circular bay. Our trucks parked near the docks, and we had a good view of the imposing white buildings, which were built on the slope that gradually rose to about 500 feet. At the top, there used to be an old fortress that is now the Casbah section of Algiers.

We discovered that there were a lot of U.S. Army personnel in the city because it had become a large supply base. It was here that we found out that there were women in the U.S. Army. We saw our first WAC! After talking to the WAC, a group of us went to a bar called the Kit Kat Club. Each of us bought a bottle of champagne.

Later Sgt. McFarland and I became separated from the rest of the group. We had been talking about the movie *Algiers* which had Charles Boyer playing

A map of the Mediterranean area.

the Paris thief Pepe le Moko, who had been hiding from the police in the Casbah section of Algiers. We decided to see what the Casbah looked like. After a while, things got quite confusing. We were not used to drinking champagne, and it affected our judgment. Some time later, we were on the second floor of an old rundown building, and four or five Arabs were giving us a hard time about something. It was a tense situation, according to McFarland, although I don't remember it. I reached in back under my field jacket, where I always carried a hunting knife in a sheath attached to my belt. I pulled the knife out and stated calmly, "You people didn't know I had this, did you?"

At that moment, an uproar started, and McFarland and I ran down the stairs with the Arabs in pursuit. As we came out the door, we ran right into the arms of two MPs who happened to be patrolling the area. Our pursuers made a quick exit, and the MPs admonished us for being in an "off-limits area" and returned us to our trucks.

May 16, 1943. Orléansville, Algeria

We left L'Arba early the next morning and traveled by vehicle 130 miles to Orléansville (El Asnam), arriving at 1700 hours, and bivouacked. This was just a pause in our long trip back to Oran, Algeria.

May 17–20, 1943. Sidi Chami, Algeria

We left Orleansville and traveled 133 miles to Sidi Chami and bivouacked. This was to be a permanent camp until we had a new mission.

One thing I learned in Tunisia was that the infantrymen had decidedly unromantic lives. They fought, they waited, they endured dive bombing, shelling, cold, heat, bugs, rain, snow, and they died. As Ernie Pyle said about the infantryman, after he spent time with the 1st Division, "They were heroes, not dashing or even particularly brave, but men who persisted in the face of great fear and discomfort because they had to."*

*In Ernie's War: The Best of Ernie Pyle's World War II Dispatches (New York: Simon and Schuster, 1987), page 18.

Nine

Sicily

May 21–31, 1943. Sidi Chami, Algeria

The aid station was set up but was only used for the company sick call because we were in a rest area. We were now performing the usual camp duties. Clothing, medical equipment and other supplies were replenished. Most of the ambulances had bullet and shell holes and required maintenance so they would be ready for the next operation. One of our enterprising ambulance drivers found an unattended ambulance and brought it back to the company. We now had 13 ambulances, while some other medical unit had to account for a missing ambulance.

The men were given passes, and recreational convoys went to the various cities and towns. These were Oran, Mascara and Sidi-Bel-Abbès. The 1st Infantry Division had a reputation for being different from other Army units, and when the division returned to the vicinity of Oran after the Tunisian battles were over, the soldiers let off steam. They caused trouble with some of the supply and other noncombat units. This was called the second battle of Oran.

The division commander winked at this lack of discipline. He thought the men were owed some fun and relaxation. The assistant division commander, General Roosevelt, felt the same way and said the 1st Division was an assault unit and needed high morale in order to keep its edge.

The headquarters of the French Foreign Legion was located in Sidi-Bel-Abbès. About six months ago, we had been fighting the French and now we were allies. Sidi-Bel-Abbès was an interesting little city. It seemed to be more of an army garrison than a city. On one occasion, when I was there, the time came to lower the flag (called Retreat). A band played the "Marseillaise," and all Allied troops came to attention. After a short pause, the band played "God Save the King," and again all troops came to attention. Finally, after another pause, "The Star Spangled Banner" was played, and all soldiers again stood at attention. I suppose the same thing would happen in the morning when the colors were raised.

There were several moving picture theaters in Sidi-Bel-Abbès where we could see old moving pictures in French or in English with French subtitles. It was a typical army garrison city.

June 1, 1943. Mangin, Algeria

The company left Sidi Chami at 0800 hours by truck and traveled four miles to an area one mile east of Mangin at 1000 hours and bivouacked. This was one of those moves that made me wonder if the Army knew what it was doing. The company would move a few miles and wait.

June 2–14, 1943. La Macta Forest, Algeria

The company left Mangin and arrived at La Macta forest at 1030 hours. La Macta was near the coast. We were here to participate in landing maneuvers. We were now training for the next operation. Some of our ambulances were sent to the 18th Infantry battalions to evacuate any men that might get injured in the maneuvers. A great deal of time was spent practicing landing from small LCVP (landing craft vehicle personnel) assault boats and in the evacuation of casualties from shore to ship using amphibious trucks. When we had spare time, we were kept busy with calisthenics, road marches and classes on first aid. It was my job to conduct the first aid classes.

June 15–23, 1943. Port aux Poules, Algeria

We left La Macta at 1030 hours and traveled by truck ten miles arriving at 1130, hours and bivouacked. The area was near Arzew, a port of debarkation. The landing maneuvers continued.

June 24, 1943. Aboard an LCI (landing craft infantry)

The company split up. The ambulances and trucks, with the drivers, were loaded on either cargo ships or LSTs (landing ship tanks). Most of our litter bearers were with the battalions of the 18th Infantry on other landing craft. The aid station platoon and company headquarters left Port aux Poules by truck, went to the port of Arzew and boarded an LCI. We were carrying vest haversacks, which were filled with medical supplies, as well as our standard combat equipment. This meant we would be on an assault landing somewhere. We left for an unknown destination at 2300 hours.

The LCI that I was on carried a unit of the 18th Infantry as well as our small group. An LCI is about 150 feet long and carries about 200 men. It is constructed with two ramps, one on each side of the bow, which can be lowered into the water. When we go in for a landing, the LCI goes in toward the shore as far as possible, and then one end of each ramp is lowered into the water. The soldiers then go down the ramps into the water and wade ashore.

We were crowded on the LCI. The bunks were four high, and the top one was close to the ceiling of the compartment. Because the LCI has to get in as close to shore as possible, the bottom of the vessel is flat. Because of this, the LCIs didn't ride the waves as well as most other ships. In rough weather, they rocked and pitched rather violently, and many soldiers would get seasick.

June 25–27, 1943. At sea in the Mediterranean

The first day was pleasant and relaxing. The weather was good, and the food was tremendous. This was the first time we had been on a U.S. troop ship since we left the States about a year ago. The LCI did not have a large mess hall so we ate on deck, using our own mess kits. We could even take hot showers, although we had to use hot saltwater. The Navy provided saltwater soap, which helped a little.

I noticed we were going east in the Mediterranean. We must be heading for a landing somewhere in Europe. We were hugging the coast of North Africa as we went east. I talked to the chief bosun's mate to see if he had any idea where we were going. He had no idea. He was an interesting character. He was regular Navy and had spent most of his Navy time in Asia. He loved the life in Asia and wanted to go back there. However, it did not look as if that would happen for a long time.

June 28–July 4, 1943. Carthage, Tunisia

Our LCI arrived at the entrance of the bay of Tunis on June 28. During the voyage on the LCI, we traveled about 700 miles. The LCI maneuvered to a dock, and we were told to get our gear and prepare to leave. We took our packs, which held our shelter half and a blanket, and marched six miles to an area near Carthage called La Goulette. This was the location of the Kentucky Staging Area (a staging area is where military units are collected prior to a battle). We set up our pup tents and waited, with thousands of other 1st Infantry Division men, for word to move out for the next battle. Everyone was out in the open on a large sandy plain. There was no shade except for what we could make with our shelter halves. The sun was blazing down, and the temperature would get up to 120 degrees Fahrenheit during the day.

We had to line up by the thousands for meals because all the company kitchens were loaded on cargo ships. The meals were provided by the staging area people. This is why I have very little patience to stand in line even now. Once a day, we got a drink of iced lemonade. This was one line I never missed, and everyone was ready for a cold drink. The lemonade was water flavored with a powder. I believe it was largely ascorbic acid (vitamin C).

We would know a few hours in advance if we were to move out, so a few of us would walk to the shore to cool off with a swim in the Mediterranean sea. It was a several-mile walk to the sea so it did not help much to cool off in the water because you had to walk back in the hot sun. It was interesting to watch some of the Arab women cooling off in the sea. They were all dressed up in their robes, and their faces were covered. They would walk out into the sea, and the robes would float up around them. When they were finished, they would just walk out and let the robes dry off as they stood in the sun. As for us, we would strip to our shorts and really go swimming. The water was clear and cool.

I did get a chance to explore the old Roman amphitheater and the museum at Carthage. The amphitheater was not in very good shape but it did have an inlaid mosaic floor. I was surprised to see a swastika inlaid in the tile floor in the old amphitheater. I thought the swastika was one of Hitler's ideas. A native guide, who was nearby, heard me commenting on the swastika. He told me that the swastika was one of the many Roman military and cultural names and symbols adopted by the Nazis. The museum at Carthage was full of old artifacts from the Roman era and even some from the founders of Carthage. It made me think of one place near Mateur (where we were fighting just a few months ago, about 50 miles north). Some of the men in our company had been sleeping in old Roman tombs because of the intensive German shell fire.

Father McEvoy held a service in a beautiful Catholic church in Carthage. Several of us from the station platoon and many men from the 18th Infantry attended.

July 5–6, 1943. Tunis Harbor, Tunisia

Our group left the staging area at 0600 hours, marched five miles to a dock and boarded the LCI. We stayed aboard for two days, waiting for orders.

July 7, 1943. At sea

The LCI left Tunis harbor at 0800 hours, went out to sea and then turned south. We finally came to the port of Sousse, Tunisia (about 100 miles south of Carthage). We stayed aboard for the night. We were not sure what was going on but it seemed normal to move and wait. There were more ships coming into the harbor and a huge fleet was starting to assemble.

July 8, 1943. Sousse, Tunisia

In the morning, we went ashore for a four-mile hike and returned to the LCI. We were told we would be seeing action very soon, and a lot of us went swimming off the LCI. The water was very clear, and we were all trying to dive to the bottom of the harbor. We were about 1,500 yards from shore and anchored. The water was about 20 feet deep, and I finally made bottom and picked up a rock. I wasn't so sure I could carry it all the way up but I finally succeeded.

In the afternoon, there was a great commotion on one of the LCIs. It seems that one man decided he did not want to go and was swimming ashore. Because we now knew a battle was imminent and many men knew where we were going, it was important that nobody talk to anyone on shore. The man was picked up before he got to shore.

We left Sousse just before midnight, at 2345 hours. Most of the 200 men aboard our LCI were in their bunks. The bunks in both the forward and aft compartments were stacked four high and slung from frames made from pipes that were welded to the low ceiling and the metal deck.

July 9, 1943. Aboard the LCI at sea

When I got up, I could see we were a small part of a huge convoy of warships and landing craft. It seemed like the LCIs were the smallest crafts in the armada. About noon, the sky clouded up and the sea became quite choppy. The LCI with its flat bottom did not ride very well, and many of the men were feeling seasick and were lying on their bunks. I thought the rough sea was exhilarating and stayed on deck. By late afternoon, the wind got stronger, and the chief bosun's mate said it was blowing over 35 miles per hour. The sea became very rough, and the LCI was rolling so badly it became too wet to stay on deck, so I went down to my bunk.

The evening meal was difficult to eat because we had to go to the small galley to fill our mess kits and then go back to the compartment to eat. We then had to return to wash our mess kits. Some of the men started for the galley but got seasick and immediately went back to their bunks. Others didn't even try. This made it easier for the ones that did not get sick. Some even ate in the crew's mess.

The intensity of the storm increased as night set in, and it was difficult to sleep. During the night, I was awakened by a tremendous jolt. I first thought we had been hit by a shell or torpedo, but soon word was passed to us that we had collided with another ship. No serious damage occurred, although some of the bunks were torn loose by the impact, and a few men had tumbled off them onto the deck.

July 10, 1943. Aboard the LCI near Malta

By morning, the storm had abated somewhat and, when I went on deck to look around, the visibility was excellent. However, there wasn't another ship in sight. We had lost the fleet. The young naval officer who commanded the LCI had made sure he did not collide again, and he got off course and was lost. We were somewhere near Malta.

I figured we would be an easy target for any German or Italian planes because we did not have the protection of the fleet's anti-aircraft guns. The LCI had only two-20-mm guns and several 30-caliber machine guns as defensive weapons. Not only was there little air defense and no defense against enemy submarines, but there were only four small life rafts on the LCI. They would not hold more than 50 men, and we had 200 men aboard plus the crew.

We got back on course and headed for our objective, which we now knew was the island of Sicily. We were told an armada of 2,000 vessels had already started to land troops on Sicily. The initial units of the 1st Infantry Division had landed on the high tide on July 10, 1943, at 0245 hours.

In conjunction with the troops landing by sea, there had been an air drop of 2,700 paratroopers from the 82d Airborne Division, who were supposed to land a few miles inland from the beaches where the 1st Division was to land. The paratroopers were to take the high ground behind the beach. The storm's high winds greatly affected the air drop, and the paratroopers were scattered along 60 miles of the coast of Sicily. However, the initial resistance was crushed, and the town of Gela was captured. When we finally got back to the fleet, we found that the 18th Infantry Combat Team had been kept as the floating reserve. Because the division expected a strong counterattack, the 18th Infantry Combat Team was now ordered to land as soon as possible. Our LCI stayed offshore and I watched the mine sweepers clearing lanes for the landing craft. It was dark before our LCI was given instructions to proceed toward shore. When our time came to land, we got all our gear together and lined up in position to debark. Our LCI sped in toward the assault beach. It was dark, but there was light from the moon.

When the LCI got close to shore, the crew dropped the large rear anchor. They trailed out the anchor cable, so if the LCI got stuck on a sandbar they could winch it back into deeper water. The LCI went in until it struck a sandbar and the ramps, one on each side of the bow, were let down into the rough sea. The effect of the storm we had encountered was still a problem, and the sea was running high. Even though it was night, the moonlight was bright enough so we could make out large breakers hitting the shore about 300 feet away. One of the sailors went down the ramp and jumped into the water. He said the water was only-knee deep and that it was all right to disembark.

The commander of the LCI gave the order to go ashore. As we lined up to go down the ramps, he told us the water was so shallow we should leave our life preservers in the forward hold. We went down the ramp, dropping our life preservers as we passed by the forward hold. The water was about knee-deep and even with the three-foot swells, was not very difficult to walk. This was going to be an easy landing.

However, after walking about ten feet, the bottom suddenly dropped away, and I went down into water that was over my head. With the rough sea and the heavy load I was carrying (we were all loaded down with extra gear), I had a hard time—and I am a strong swimmer. Without life preservers to give us the added buoyancy, we all had a difficult swim for 15–20 feet to another sandbar. As we neared shore, the larger swells and a strong undertow compounded our difficulty, and many men were in trouble. Finally, with everyone helping each other, all of our group got to shore safely. Not all of the 200 men on our LCI were as lucky. One officer in the 18th Infantry drowned while attempting to go ashore in the heavy sea. Later, I heard several more on our LCI also drowned. When I got ashore, I saw discarded life preservers all over the beach. Not everyone in the Navy thought that life preservers were more valuable than lives.

Our group of about 200 men gathered together a short distance from the shore. Here, we were met by the beach master, who told us to go to an assembly area on the southern slope of a hill on the eastern side of the Gela plain. Our company went inland a short distance to the rear of one of the infantry companies. We would set up the aid station when it became light.

I was beginning to feel sick, and I knew I must have a fever because my eyes were burning and my bones ached. I took a few aspirin and tried to sleep.

Later that night, 2,000 more paratroopers of the 82nd Airborne Division dropped from 144 C-47s which came from Tunisia. The time they came over was right after a German force of bombers had attacked the fleet. The fleet had put up a tremendous anti-aircraft barrage to drive off the German planes. They had just stopped when the C-47s came over and the fleet thought the paratroopers' planes were another German bomber formation. So, the fleet turned all their ant-aircraft guns on the C-47s and scattered the formation and shot a number of them down. Since our infantry thought they were German paratroopers, those that managed to get out of the planes and parachute down were in danger of being shot. Twenty-three of the C-47s were shot down and 20 percent of the paratroopers were casualties.

We had paratroopers coming into our area for about a week. However, because U.S. paratroopers were all over the area, the German and Italian troops became panicky because they thought there were more than there actually were. The paratroopers caused a lot of trouble by blowing up bridges, cutting communication lines and in general creating havoc.

July 11, 1943. Gela, Sicily

At daybreak, we were about to set up the aid station when there was a lot of gunfire, and shells were starting to land close to us. The enemy was attacking the beachhead. I was startled by an odd noise that sounded like pigs squealing. I soon found out it was our artillery shells hitting the attacking German tanks. We did not have any of our tanks here. I dived into a ravine along with the others in my platoon, and the battle progressed around us. The fleet and the beach, which was only a half mile away, were being attacked by German bombers. I was not only sick, I was scared.

When I got out of the ravine to look around, I saw General Teddy Roosevelt, the assistant division commander, calmly walking around giving orders and acting unconcerned about the situation. He was dressed, like all of us, in baggy O.D.s (olive drab uniforms) and no necktie. All he carried was a swagger stick. His demeanor calmed everyone. However, I bet he was as scared as I was. He was trying to get all available anti-tank weapons to this area. The few 105-mm field artillery guns that were ashore had their barrels horizontal and were aiming them point-blank at the German tanks.

An infantryman told me that some German tanks had broken through our lines at 0630 that morning and were heading for the beach. Twenty tanks were coming down the main road to Gela, where all the supplies were being landed, and 40 more tanks were coming towards us from another direction. Our artillery and anti-tank guns were still coming ashore, and our lightly armed infantry was being overrun by the tanks. We were lucky that the Germans did not have any infantry with them because it was easier to get out of the tank's way if they did not have infantry support.

Every available gun in the division was put into action to repulse the tanks. We had very few anti-tank guns ashore and not many artillery pieces because many had been lost when German bombers had sunk some of the cargo ships. As the artillery came off the landing craft, it was immediately put into action. At the same time, naval fire support shore parties called for help from the big guns on our warships.

The artillery, combined with the naval guns shooting at short range and the infantry using all the weapons at their disposal, repulsed the tank attack, and the positions were restored. Half of the 60 German tanks were destroyed in this fierce battle. The remaining German tanks withdrew. However, we knew that enemy reinforcements were arriving all along the division front. The following is from an account by General Bradley about this battle:

> The Herman Goering Panzer Division had attacked the First Division down the Gela road with its tanks to throw the U.S. back into the sea. I question if any other U.S. division could have repelled the attack in time to save the beach from tank penetration. Only the perverse Big Red One with its no less perverse commander was hard and experienced enough to take that assault in stride. A greener division might easily have panicked. On April 23, Patton had asked Eisenhower to substitute the veteran 1st Division for the 36th on this invasion of Sicily. By doing so, he may have saved the II Corps from a major disaster.*

After the casualties were evacuated and things became a little quieter I began to realize I was quite sick. I took my temperature, and it was over 104. I was burning up with fever and out of drinking water. Each of us had been issued two canteens prior to the landing because it was felt drinking water would be scarce. The only place to get a refill of water was on the beach. We did not have any vehicles ashore, so I walked about a half mile to the beach, where the fleet was unloading reinforcements and equipment.

I had no sooner filled my canteens from a five-gallon water can that had been preloaded on an amphibious truck when a group of German bombers came over and bombed the fleet. With all the flack going up and the bombs coming down, it was a hot place, so I dived into an empty hole. Several men dived on top of me. I did not mind because they gave me a little more protection. The bombers hit one freighter, and it started to burn and eventually sank.

When the German planes left, I went back to the aid station, where it seemed much safer. After taking more aspirin, I managed to stay effective. My fever subsided in about three days. The fever was diagnosed as dengue fever, or commonly called sand fly fever.

Later that evening, the 18th Combat Team moved about five miles. We were all on foot because many vehicles had been lost when the ships were sunk. The German air raids had also delayed the unloading of cargo ships.

July 12, 1943. Vicinity of Gela, Sicily

A night patrol had observed 20 German trucks unloading infantry reinforcements with four or five tanks in support. It looked as if they were preparing to attack in the morning. The division beat them to it. The division attacked at 0350 hours. The 1st Division had learned in North Africa that night attacks, difficult to perform, were very effective against the Germans.

*Omar N. Bradley, A Soldier's Story (New York: Henry Holt, 1951), page 130.

It succeeded here. The Ponte Olivo airport and the high ground near it was captured. Many prisoners were taken and at least five tanks were destroyed. We found out later that the unit opposing us was the Hermann Goering Panzer Division. Many in the division had panicked because of the night attack.

The aid station was set up and operating. We now had a jeep and three ambulances ashore. Transport K-40 had been sunk on July 11, and we lost three of our ambulances on the ship. Two of our men on K-40 reported for duty. The other man was also safe but was not with the other two. One of the ambulances lost was the one we had found abandoned in Algeria. Someone has an unsolvable mystery of a missing ambulance.

The 1st Infantry Division was now reinforced by part of the 2d Armored Division. We were also receiving help from the paratroopers of the 82d Airborne Division. They had been scattered behind the German and Italian lines and were taking whatever action they could to disrupt the enemy. Some of them stayed with the division for a while.

July 13–14, 1943. Gela (3½ miles north), Sicily

The aid station was operating, and we had enough vehicles ashore to be in complete operation.

T5 Gosselin had been wounded. He was an ambulance driver who had been on transport K-40 when it was sunk on July 11. He received a lacerated wound from a shell or bomb fragment.

The division had now secured the high ground around Gela. This consisted of Mt. Figaro, Mt. Conolotti and Mt. Gibilscemi. All resistance in the area had been subdued. Now our air force could use the Ponte-Olivo airport. Mazzarino was captured on July 14.

July 15, 1943. Gela (16 miles north), Sicily

The aid station and ambulances were in operation. We moved 9½ miles from the last location by vehicle. The infantry was not as fortunate. They had to walk because so many of their trucks had been lost. The infantry walked a lot in Sicily.

July 16, 1943. Mazzarino, Sicily

We moved ten miles by vehicle. The aid station was set up and in operation.

There were many German counterattacks by tank-supported infantry to try and prevent the capture of Barrafranca. The enemy force consisted of the 15th Panzer Division, the 71st Nebelwerfer Battalion and the 382d Infantry Regiment. The Nebelwerfers were large-caliber rockets (150- and 210-mm) and were particularly unnerving because of the large shells that they hurled and the screaming noise they made when they came in on their target. When a large concentration is fired in one area, it can be devastating. The defense is good holes and quick artillery counterfire. We used the 155-mm howitzers and in Sicily, we had some Long Toms (155-mm. long-barreled artillery) attached to the division. They were very effective against the Nebelwerfers.

July 17–18, 1943. Piazza Armerina, Sicily

The aid station was set up and operating. The Allied plan to secure Sicily and to trap the maximum number of enemy troops was for the British forces to capture Messina by going north up the east coast of Sicily. They were to keep Mt. Etna on their left as they advanced north. The U.S. forces would take the western part of the island, which included Palermo. The 1st Infantry Division was to attack north through the center of Sicily.

The south coast of Sicily is a drab, light-brown color and is somewhat flat until you get about a mile inland. At that point, some good-sized hills start to rise. As you travel farther inland or north from Gela, it gets mountainous, and the mountains rise up in steep cliffs. The towns are, for the most part, crowded into the valleys, and many of the mountains are terraced for the growing of fruits and vegetables. The people seem to live in the towns rather than adjacent to the gardens. In general, the people are poor. The houses were all old and needed repair. We would see the women on the banks of the streams, washing clothes. They would use the rocks on the sides of the streams to scrub their clothes.

There are not many roads through the mountainous center of the island. However, there are many bridges on these roads because they are needed to span the streams and ravines, which are plentiful in this rugged territory. The Germans and Italians blocked the roads at strategic passes and bridges. They would also fortify the high ground near the passes and bridge sites. When the enemy felt they could no longer hold the bridges, they would blow up the bridges. Then, using their strong defensive positions, they would make it difficult and costly for our infantry to secure the opposite side of the bridge site. When the bridge site was captured, the engineers would have to repair the crossing. I say repair the crossing because sometimes the engineers would not repair the bridge but would just fill the ravine by using bulldozers to scrape fill from the surrounding area.

Without the means to cross the rivers or ravines, our tanks, ambulances and trucks could not be used to transport or supply the infantry. The infantry would have to bypass the enemy strong points near the bridges by going over the mountains on foot and fighting for the strategic high ground. Then they could direct artillery and mortar fire on the enemy strong points to aid them as they assaulted the bridge sites. Thus, the battle in Sicily was a succession of short, fierce battles for the high ground. The infantry had to go up the hills, cliffs and trails, which were impassable for even jeeps. At times, mules had to be used to bring up supplies or, in a few cases, supplies were air-dropped. The support units, artillery, engineers, armored units and, of course, our aid station and ambulances had to travel on the roads and would keep as close as possible to the infantry.

On July 18, the division crossed the Salso river in a night attack and seized the high ground on the other side. The bridge had been blown, and a fierce battle was fought over the bridge site, with our forces prevailing. The 1st Engineer Battalion had to prepare a crossing for the tanks, trucks and ambulances. We then crossed over and set up our aid station to evacuate the casualties.

July 19, 1943. Caltanissetta, Sicily

We moved by vehicle and set up the aid station in the city. Caltanissetta, the provincial capital, is a large city. The people seemed to be friendly even though we were their enemy. Perhaps the Italians had had enough of the war.

Whenever we set up our aid station near a large village or city in Sicily, we would have older Sicilian men stop in and talk to us. They could speak English well, and most of them claimed they used to work in the States when they were younger. When they saved enough money, they would come back to Sicily, get married and live the life of a rich man.

The 18th Infantry went through Caltanissetta and captured Villarosa.

July 20–23, 1943. Villarosa, Sicily

We moved by vehicle, the aid station was set up, and we were evacuating casualties. On July 20, Enna was captured but, because of a blown bridge, tanks could not be used to aid the infantry in reconnoitering, and our advance was slowed down.

The roads here were so steep that we sometimes had to go up the mountains in low gear. One time, as we were going up a mountain road, a Sicilian was coming down in his two wheeled wagon pulled by a donkey. The donkey got scared by all the vehicles and started running down the steep road. The donkey lost his footing, slipped and fell and started sliding down the hill on his side, pulling the wagon and driver. The last I saw of them was a frightened

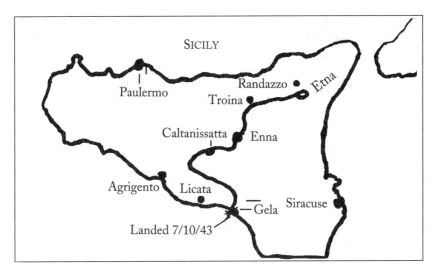

The route of the 18th RCT in Sicily from Gela to Enna, Troina and Randazzo.

man jumping off his wagon and the donkey and wagon still sliding down the steep hill.

The British 8th Army under General Montgomery was having trouble in its attack toward Messina. In order to help the British, the U.S. II Corps was directed to shift its attack to the east toward Troina. The capture of Troina would cut off the enemy troops in western Sicily. It would also open up the northern approach to Messina.

July 24, 1943. Gaia (3 miles south), Sicily

We set up the station and were evacuating casualties. Every time we set up the aid station near any habitation, we seem to attract a few civilians who need some medical attention. This time, we had a fellow about 35-40 years old come in very disturbed. I could not understand him because he did not speak English, and no one in the aid station could speak Italian. He kept opening his mouth and pointing inside. I got a flashlight and looked in his mouth and throat. After a careful examination, I saw a small, black snake-like tail swishing back and forth behind his epiglottis. I did not know what it was.

We found one of the ambulance drivers, who could speak Italian. He talked to the Italian, and the man said it was a leech attached to his throat. Apparently, in Sicily, they sometimes have leeches in the drinking water. The leech, when it was very small, went in with a drink of water and attached itself to his throat. It had been there for several months, growing bigger all the time.

The man had been one miserable person because every time it wiggled it made him feel sick. One of our doctors decided to try to help him. He used a long hemostat and, with a great deal of patience, managed to grab the leech and pull it off. The patient was one happy Sicilian.

I decided never to drink any water in Sicily unless it had been filtered and purified at our water points. The 1st Engineer Battalion provides drinking water for the combat team. An engineer will scout the surrounding areas, looking for watering places. When a water point is found, they set up a portable purifying unit, consisting of a pump, a sand filter, a chlorinating machine and a 3,000 gallon canvas tank. Purified water is kept in the tank, and the combat team fills its water cans and water trailers from this tank.

July 25–27, 1943. Gangi (3 miles southwest), Sicily

The aid station was set up and operating as usual. On July 24, the 4th Tabor of 280 Goums was attached to the 18th Infantry Combat Team to help fight in these rugged mountains. The Goums were a native French Moroccan unit. They were from the Atlas mountains and were used to this type of terrain. A few of them were wounded and passed through our aid station during the next few days. They spoke French, and I believe they were a Free French unit. They seemed to be excellent soldiers and did a lot of night fighting. Their specialty was to infiltrate the enemy lines. We were told they used knives at night to kill the enemy sentries. They would then cut off their ears and bring them back as proof of their success.

July 28, 1943. Gangi (4 miles east), Sicily

Gangi was not very far from the north coast of Sicily. This meant we were close to cutting the Germans' line of communication to the west. This was very mountainous terrain. On the way, we were forced to stop and wait until a German tank could either be knocked out or be forced to move. The tank was in a position where it could shell our route of travel. We were on one side of a deep ravine, and the tank was firing at trucks of our convoy winding up the mountain on the other side of the ravine.

While we were stopped, I heard the German tank fire one shot. The tank seemed to be above and behind us. I could see the shell hit directly behind one of the trucks. A few seconds later, I heard another shot, and a shell hit ahead of the truck. When the German tank fired the third time, it was a direct hit to the truck's cargo. I saw the driver ditch the truck and jump out. He was lucky because it was an ammunition truck. It started burning, and the cargo kept exploding like firecrackers. When the tank was finally knocked out, the truck was pushed off the road by a bulldozer, and we continued on our way.

We got to the new area and set up the aid station and proceeded to evacuate the casualties we had been accumulating. The problem was that the German tank had stopped traffic on our single road. One of the seriously wounded men we were holding was an aid man from A Company of the 1st Medical Battalion. He had a bad head wound and was unconscious and was continually thrashing his arms. I did not think he would live.

It was very hard to get supplies to the infantry, who were on the high ground away from the roads. Mules and carrying parties were being used to supply the soldiers as they walked over the mountains. It was also difficult to get wounded men out as they had to be taken out by litter bearers or on the backs of mules. We heard that they were even flying mules in from the States to help in the battle.

Nicosia was captured on July 28, and most of what was left of the Italian Aosta Division deserted. The 18th captured 700 Italian soldiers along with a few Germans.

July 29–August 1, 1943. Nicosia (8 miles southeast), Sicily

Again, we had another delay as a bridge was blown. This had become a series of battles for the mountain tops. The weather was hot, and the infantrymen were continually walking up and down the barren mountains. They were having difficulty getting food, water and ammunition. Many of them were now coming down with malaria. While we all were taking Atabrine (as a prophylactic) to prevent malaria, I suspect a lot of the infantrymen had not been able to get a continuous supply. We were seeing more and more infantrymen with extremely high fevers (105 and even 106). Later, they would have chills. Even when the air temperature was 90, the men with chills could not be kept warm and would shake violently. I still remember the odor of men who had been sweating from both fear and high fever and who were not able to even wash their faces.

The men with malaria were extremely thirsty. One time, a soldier with malaria came into the aid station and went right to our red water can. We painted it red to warn everyone not to drink it. This is where we kept our USP alcohol. The man, thinking it was water, filled his canteen cup and took a big swallow. He was shocked and perhaps not unhappy, at least later. We gave him water as a chaser.

On July 31, the attack for Troina started. The battle for Troina was the toughest and most significant of the Sicilian campaign. Troina was situated on the top of a 3,600-foot peak and was an important road junction. One

German battle group had dug itself in for a "do or die" stand on excellent defensive terrain. The enemy occupied the high ground north, west and south of Troina. They used the town itself as an observation post and as an artery of supply and communication. It was very important for the Germans to hold Troina as long as possible in order to protect their withdrawal over the straits at Messina. This was their only means of escape to the mainland of Italy.

We had nine battalions of artillery firing on the German positions. This would be 108 guns, and they fired 5,500 shells the first day. The mountains were so steep that it looked like our artillery was firing straight up in the air. The Germans responded by bombing Nicosia with Messerschmitt-109s and Focke-Wulf-190s. We did not have any casualties from the bombing.

August 2, 1943. Cerami (4 miles northwest), Sicily

We set up the aid station and were operating as usual. The Germans also had heavy concentrations of artillery in Troina and were giving us a lot of return fire. The 15th Panzer Division had units dug in over all the strategic high ground.

August 3–5, 1943. Gagliano, Sicily

The 18th Infantry Combat Team's mission, along with the rest of the 1st Division, was to take the strategic hills and finally capture Troina. Again, there were night attacks and, many times, all weapons had to be carried in rough terrain. It seemed to me that the small, wiry men were always the ones carrying the heavy mortar base plates or the heavy machine guns and mortar barrels. They must have more stamina than the big men.

To take one major objective, fierce hand-to-hand fighting took place, and both sides had heavy casualties. We noticed that the types of wounds were different. Normally, the infantrymen would have more shell fragment wounds than gunshot wounds. In this action, we saw more gunshot wounds and even bayonet wounds. There were also almost continuous artillery barrages on Troina as well as air attacks by flights of A-36s. By August 5, the 18th Infantry had secured an excellent observation point which looked into the enemy's gun positions and our artillery knocked out many of its guns.

August 6–13, 1943. Troina (2 miles northeast), Sicily

On August 6, Troina was captured. After clearing out mines, the 18th Infantry advanced to Randazzo and Mojo Rocca Bodia. The advance was slow because of blown-out bridges and extensive fields of Teller, Box and S mines.

August 14, 1943. Randazzo (2½ miles northwest), Sicily

Randazzo was a small hill city on the slopes of Mt. Etna (10,750 ft.). It was a medieval city and full of lava dust. Etna was always smoking and spewing out black lava dust or soot. At night, you could see the glow of the molten lava. I always felt dirty around Etna, and I believe everyone was dirty although it may have been because we hadn't had a shower since early July.

August 15–19, 1943. Mojo (2½ miles west; 2 miles from Randazzo), Sicily

The 18th Infantry Combat Team reached the road junction of the Francavilla-Novara roads. We occupied Novara on the 15th without resistance and took 150 Italian prisoners and much equipment and stores.

As other divisions were pushing toward Messina, the 1st Division action ended on August 16, 1943. The official end of the Sicilian campaign was August 17, 1943. In 37 days of continuous fighting, the division had taken 18 towns and captured 5,935 prisoners. The number of casualties in Sicily was much less than in North Africa. The 18th Infantry Combat Team had three officers and 50 men killed, 11 officers and 253 men wounded and 34 missing in action. The 1st Division total casualties were 267 killed in action, 1,184 wounded and 337 missing in action.

Mines had been a big problem and had caused many casualties. The 1st Engineer Battalion had repaired or made bypasses on 39 bridges and had removed thousands of mines. In one area near Randazzo, there was a 12-mile stretch where they could not use mine detectors. The iron content of the lava from Mt. Etna made the mine detectors useless. These mines took much longer to remove because the engineers had to probe by hand for them.

The physical abuse of the infantry was bad. Ernie Pyle said, "The infantry reaches a stage of exhaustion that is incomprehensible to you folks back home. The men in the First Division for instance were in the lines twenty-eight days, walking and fighting all that time day and night."[*]

The aid station was set up in Randazzo but, as there was no action, we only had to take care of the sick. We stayed there a few days waiting for

*In Ernie's War (1987), page 153.

orders. At night, we could see the red glow of the hot lava reflect against the clouds. During the day, the grimy volcanic dust combined with the hot August sun made it difficult to even keep our hands and faces clean. We were now in a temporary camp, waiting for orders. However, even then you could be in danger. During one of the meals, I was talking with Father McEvoy when a bullet hit the fender of a trailer less than a foot from us. The bullet went through the fender and deep into the ground. I dug it out of the ground and saw it was a 50-caliber bullet. It probably was a spent bullet fired from a plane, but it could have hurt someone.

Ten

Sicilian Interlude

August 20–October 19, 1943. Palma
(3 miles southeast), Sicily

On August 20 (my 23d birthday), we moved from Mojo (by truck) and traveled 167 miles to Palma and bivouacked. Palma is on the south coast of Sicily and not far from Gela, where we first landed. Palma (the full name is Palma di Montechiaro) is about halfway between Gela and Agrigento.

Our company camped in a grove of almond trees on the south coast of Sicily. There was a sandy beach on the Mediterranean about 100 yards from our area. It was a very pleasant location. When we were told that this location was to be our semi-permanent camp, Sgt. McFarland and I set up our two shelter halves under an almond tree. We would be here for the next two months.

An almond tree is about 10–12 feet tall and gives quite a bit of shade. There were enough trees so that every tent could have its own tree. Each almond tree had many large nuts growing on them, and it looked like they soon would be ready for picking.

We proceeded to clean up. Everyone really needed a shower because we had not been able to take one since early July. It would be nice to wash off the accumulation of sweat and black volcanic dust from Mt. Etna. Some of the men heated water up to the boiling point to wash their uniforms. We were still wearing heavy woolen uniforms in Sicily. I understand that the division commander had asked for the lighter khaki uniforms, but General Patton thought the 1st Division ought to sweat more.

The woolen uniforms shrunk so bad that the soldiers could not wear them. They were forced to get new uniforms, which were not faded. Most men did not like this. The way you identified a recruit from a veteran was a new man always had a new uniform and a veteran had a faded uniform. I decided to be smart and dry-cleaned mine by soaking it in gasoline. However, this was a mistake. Even though I dried and aired my uniform all day in the sun, I still got quite a burn from the retained gasoline vapors.

We then had to restock medical supplies and replace worn equipment.

Our ambulances were quite a sight because all of them had either bullet holes or shell holes in them. It was a good thing that wounded men don't really look at the vehicles they ride in or they might have thought the ambulances were not safe.

To keep busy, we had to start regular training all over again. This consisted of classes, road marches, organized athletics. etc. We did have to continue our medical duties and send ambulances to the infantry battalions so the sick could be transported to the 15th Evacuation Hospital. We also had to set up for our own sick call. An additional duty arose for the station platoon because the men in the combat team were still coming down with malaria and other tropical diseases. We had to set up and vaccinate many of the men of the combat team and give booster shots for typhus, yellow fever and tetanus. This took a long time because we would have hundreds of men in line and had to keep sterilizing the needles. We even had to stop and sharpen them.

It's surprising to see an infantryman who has performed bravely in battle become frightened when it comes to having a needle stuck in him. We sometimes would get a man who would be shivering so badly that two men would have to hold him while the shot was administered. In a way, I cannot blame them because we did not have a tremendous quantity of needles, and after multiple uses they did become dull.

There was plenty of time for recreation. We had one big party for the entire company. The company cooks prepared Spam sandwiches and provided whatever other goodies they could get from the division quartermaster. They also made a punch using powdered lemonade and water. My platoon then fortified the punch by adding USP alcohol. The main star of the party was a large goose that one of the ambulance drivers had picked up and kept as a pet. The goose was very friendly and must have thought he was human. He would greet everyone with a honk and wanted to be petted. The goose did have a problem. He liked to drink wine. Soon after the goose joined the party, he was so drunk he was staggering all over the area. The next morning the goose was missing. A few days later we found its skeleton nearby. Someone had been hungry for fresh fowl.

We were allowed to go to places like Agrigento and occasionally to Palermo. I went on one of the early trips to Agrigento, one of the old Greek cities in Sicily. We had lunch there at a former German officers' mess, and they still had Hitler's picture on the wall. We were served by the same Sicilians who had served the Germans. I suppose the war was just an interlude for them, and they did not care who was in control.

The temples in Agrigento did not suffer any damage from the war. One of the old temples, Jupiter, was in excellent shape. Years later, I visited Greece and the temples in Agrigento had aged much better than the ones in Athens. We were real tourists in Agrigento because we had a Sicilian guide who could talk English. He even took us into the catacombs of the old city.

On August 27, the entire division was summoned to hear an address by the 7th Army commander, Lt. Gen. George S. Patton. Our division had no love for Patton because our first experience with him had been in southern Tunisia when he took over the II Corps. He had decided to instill discipline and had ordered us all to wear ties and leggings while the division was fighting in the African desert. This did not set well with the men.

We were trucked to a natural outdoor arena formed by a small hill overlooking a level area. Here, a small platform had been constructed. While the 18,000 men were assembling, I wondered why we were there. We had been on alert because it was thought that the surrender of Italy was imminent. There was a tentative plan to land a U.S. division at the Rome airport and help to bring an earlier end to the war. Rumor had it that the 1st Division would be doing this. Did it mean the rumors were true, that we were to be airlifted to the Rome airport? We knew that the Italians wanted to get out of the war. Or was it possible that some of us might go home? After all, we had been overseas for more than a year.

The division band played while everyone was assembling. Then, an honor guard, made up of a spruced-up infantry platoon, performed a formal rifle drill. Finally, Gen. Patton was introduced by Gen. Andrus. Patton came forward, wearing his pearl-handled revolvers and his helmet liner with the three stars. He started his speech by saying, "You are part of the Seventh Army that was born at sea and baptized with the blood of our filthy enemy. We have killed many of them and will have the opportunity to kill more. That is what our job is. We are here to kill the enemy."

It was a real blood-and-guts speech. When he finished, there was complete silence. There was no applause. Nothing at all. My reaction, which was probably shared by everyone, was *What is this all about? Why are we here listening to this?* Most of us thought the speech was in bad taste. There were very few men who just wanted to kill the enemy. We would rather that they surrender so we could all go home.

It was not until weeks later that we found out what the speech was all about. I read in an old issue *Newsweek* that Patton had slapped a 1st Infantry Division soldier in a field hospital for being a coward. The man was in the hospital because he had an anxiety state breakdown, probably brought on by malaria. Patton had been ordered by Gen. Eisenhower to apologize to the men of the 1st Division. That speech was supposed to be an apology.

A few days later, in the same place, we saw a show with Bob Hope and Frances Langford. It was much better than the speech about blood and guts by Gen. Patton.

I went to an outside movie shortly after we arrived in Palma. While waiting for the movie to start, we had to fight the mosquitoes. They would attack us in droves, and they were so bad that we had to put netting over our helmets. The movie was *Sea Wolf*. This was the third time I had been to a movie and each time it was *Sea Wolf.* I saw it in Algeria, Tunisia and now Sicily. The Army must only have one movie.

On September 18, our unit was inspected by the new division commander, Maj. Gen. Clarence R. Huebner. Gen. Bradley had removed both Gen. Allen and Gen. Roosevelt because he thought they had made the 1st Infantry Division too independent. He did not think it had proper discipline. His reason for thinking this was the trouble the men of the division had caused in Oran after the Tunisian campaign had ended. He selected Gen. Huebner because he was a flinty disciplinarian. Gen. Huebner had served in the 1st Division in World War I. He had come in as a private and had served in every rank until he left as a colonel. However, we heard that Huebner was also a maverick like Allen and Roosevelt.

On the whole, the two months spent resting in Sicily was somewhat enjoyable, but the time dragged and most of us were bored. A lot of us did not feel topnotch. Perhaps we all had a touch of malaria or some other tropical disease we had picked up in Africa or Sicily. The doctors did not know what it was. We all called it the Sicilian Crud. We did not get much sympathy from the doctors. I don't think they felt so good either. All the doctors seemed to agree that if healthy people like us got sick, 90 percent of us will get better if the doctor does nothing. He can't help 5 percent, and only 5 percent can be helped. So why bother to do anything?

On October 12, we saw a division firepower demonstration. It was quite spectacular and showed the effect of all the weapons being fired at one time. The demonstration started by just firing rifles. They then added machine guns, then mortars and, finally, field artillery.

The two months were a good rest. The weather was pleasant, and the swimming was excellent, though the undertow was severe at times. One time I was out in the sea alone. When I tried to get back to shore, I found I was unable to swim toward shore and was swept parallel to the shore. I went with the current and finally got to shore about a mile away. I now saw how heavily loaded soldiers could easily drown in this water.

Our almond trees had a good harvest, and we collected the nuts in our helmets and had almond feasts. The local civilians, who probably owned the almond orchard, were selling almond candy. The candy looked and tasted good, but it made me sick. The Sicilians would also trade fresh vegetables for our food. Our cooks would trade the used coffee grounds for fresh vegetables. Coffee was a prize to the Sicilians.

My main problems were the mosquitoes and the centipedes. The mosquitoes were so bad that we were issued netting to go over each pup tent. At night, if you did not want to get bites all over your body, you would have to retreat to your tent. However, in the tent, the centipedes would crawl into the blankets at night. I would wake up feeling a wriggling clammy creature on my body. I would quickly grab it and heave it out. I understand they can give bad bites but I never was bitten by one.

October 20, 1943. Palma (3 miles southeast), Sicily

We broke camp and prepared to move to a destination unknown.

October 21, 1943. Augusta, Sicily

We left Palma at 0415 hours by motor convoy, traveled 120 miles and arrived at a staging area at Augusta, Sicily, at 1145 hours. We left our vehicles at the staging area. I heard that we were turning them in to be issued to another unit. I hope they fixed all the shell holes before they reissued the vehicles.

We left the staging area at 1730 and marched three-quarters of a mile to a dock. Then we were ferried by small boats to a troop ship in the harbor. It was the HMS *Maloja*, a British troop transport. We boarded the ship at 2045 hours. Perhaps we were going back to England to prepare for the invasion of Europe.

I expect Gen. Bradley wanted to use the 1st Infantry Division in his next operation because he had said, "In quality the First Infantry Division was worth the equal of several inexperienced divisions. It had become an almost irreplaceable weapon for the Normandy Invasion."[*]

October 22–24, 1943. Aboard the HMS Maloja, *Augusta, Sicily*

We left the port of debarkation at 1130 hours and sailed for a destination unknown. We were guessing and hoping it was England. I was quite sure we would not be going back to the States because there was a lot of war left in this part of the world. I did not expect we would go back to the States until the war was over. The *Maloja* was about the same size as the *Ettrick*, and the accommodations were about the same. We slept in hammocks, and there was more room than in an LCI. We started the usual ship duties of calisthenics, sick call and basic training classes. This is how the Army keeps people busy.

We were back on a British troop ship so we again were eating their rations. Although, just as we left Sicily, we received an unexpected present. We were each issued six cans of American beer. We were hoarding our beer like it was a treasure. Then we heard that a visiting U.S. congressional group was upset that American troops had beer issued to them. We were told to return the unused cans. In a few minutes, there were only empties to be found.

*A Soldier's Story *(1951), page 154.

Sometimes it is hard to understand the actions of our elected officials. They must believe that they have superior knowledge of what is best for everyone.

October 25–27, 1943. *Aboard the* HMS Maloja

The *Maloja* arrived at the port of Algiers at 1600 hours on the 25th. No one was allowed to leave the ship during the few days we spent in port.

We sailed from Algiers at 1630 hours on October 27. Our ship was now part of a larger convoy, and our destination was still unknown.

October 28–November 4, 1943. *Aboard the* HMS Maloja

I was sure we were leaving the Mediterranean because we were heading west. We could not be heading for immediate combat because we were not loaded for an assault landing. When we passed Gibraltar and entered the Atlantic, we turned north. I was now quite sure we were going back to England.

The voyage was uneventful and boring. I spent most of my free time reading and playing cards. On the 3d of November, we entered the waters around the United Kingdom. After passing between the U.K. and Ireland, we proceeded to go up the Mersey river. This leads to the port of Liverpool.

I had quite a scare when we started up the Mersey river channel because I could see a periscope coming down the channel towards us. None of the seamen were excited, so I assume it was a common sight. It must have been a British submarine.

November 5, 1943. *Aboard the* HMS Maloja, *Liverpool, England*

We arrived at Liverpool at 0400 hours and docked at the Mersey river docks at 1000 hours. We got all our gear together in preparation to disembark.

Eleven

Back in England

November 6, 1943. Liverpool, England

We ate breakfast at 0230 and disembarked from the HMS *Maloja* at 0430 hours. We then marched to a railway station. Here, a troop train was waiting, and we boarded at 0630 hours. The train left the station at 0715 hours. It is interesting to notice the time we ate breakfast and disembarked and how much time we spent just waiting. After a while, dates and times became meaningless.

The train traveled south from Liverpool. About noon, it stopped at a railroad station. We were able to get out and stretch. British women had set up tables at the station and served a cafeteria-style lunch. At 1700 hours, the train arrived at Maiden Newton in Dorset, England, and we detrained. The distance traveled from Liverpool was about 250 miles. There were trucks waiting for us, and after a four mile ride, we arrived at the Warden Hill Camp, Evershot, Dorset, England. Warden Hill was a British army camp, and our company occupied one of the barracks. Meals were provided by a British army unit. The rations were British and the NCOs ate in a separate mess from the rest of the enlisted men. This is not usual in the U.S. Army and at first seemed a little awkward. I soon got used to it.

November 7–14, 1943. Warden Hill Camp,
*   Evershot, Dorset, England*

On November 11, 1943, the company was reorganized under a new table of organization. There was not much change except most of the positions were raised in rank and pay. It was at this time I was promoted to T3. This is equivalent to staff sergeant and is a technical specialty. I was now a surgical technician.

New vehicles and equipment were issued at this location. This is the third time we were issued new vehicles since I was with the company. We were now fully equipped for combat.

November 15, 1943–January 11, 1944. Piddlehinton
Barracks, Dorchester, Dorset, England

The company left the Warden Hill Camp at 1010 hours on November 15 and moved, using our new company vehicles. We arrived at Piddlehinton Barracks at 1100 hours. It was only a ten-mile trip. On the way, we noticed that there were U.S. soldiers stationed all over this part of England. It was beginning to look as if most of the U.S. troops were concentrated in the southwest part of England.

Our company was set up as an independent unit in Piddlehinton, and we proceeded to organize the camp. The company cooks were in operation for the first time since Sicily. It was an old British army barracks, and all of us were sleeping in large squad rooms which held many men. There were double-decked bunks, and we had mattress covers filled with straw as mattresses.

The camp was very close to Dorchester, a sizable town of about 10,000 people. Dorchester is the county seat of Dorset county and has good rail and bus connections to all of the United Kingdom. It is an old town and was founded by the Romans in 43 A.D. There still are remains of the old Roman wall in the town. It was ideal for us because we could visit London and other parts of England and Scotland very easily. There was even a shuttle train that went eight miles to the resort port of Weymouth. Weymouth, on the English Channel, became a favorite town for most of us, and we often went there on passes. It was a sizable place and had five or six pubs, where most of the soldiers congregated. Weymouth was situated on a colorful sweep of the southeast coastline and had a wonderful beach. However, at this time, long lines of barbed wire were strung along the beach. The wire was put up when it was thought that the Germans would attempt to invade England.

In Dorchester, we could rent bicycles and explore the small, quaint villages in Dorset County. It is surprising how many houses still had thatched roofs. Dorset county was the site of some of Thomas Hardy's novels. Hardy was born nearby at Higher Bockhampton. We did find a good fish-and-chip shop in Dorchester. It sold fried white fish and excellent French fried potatoes. They would serve the fish and chips in a cone made with old newspapers. Soon Sgt. Woods got friendly with the owner, and he provided the restaurant with large cans of katsup. Now, we not only would have our feast of fish and chips, but we would have American katsup with it.

Because there had been changes of personnel, we had to start training the new people in their new jobs. As usual, we started our basic training all over again, the old standbys of calisthenics, close-order drills and classes. My job was to conduct classes on first aid. I had given the same classes so many times that I could have conducted them in my sleep.

Along with the regular camp duties and passes, we were able to take furloughs. None of us had been able to leave the company for well over a year. I had had only one ten-day furlough in the three years I had been in the Army. It was a pleasant surprise to be able to get away from the company.

The furloughs were restricted to the U.K. Most of us had been here before, so we had many places to visit. I chose to visit Glasgow, Scotland. I first went to London, where I had to change stations, and then I get on a fast train to Scotland. London was in better shape than the last time I was there. The Germans were not bombing much, and it was pleasant to visit and not be concerned about safety. The train trip was uneventful but took a long time.

In Glasgow, the Army had taken over a hotel and set it up for soldiers on leave. We had the same old thing of many cots in a room. However, it was better than anything I had been in for a couple of years. They even had sheets on the beds. I had not slept between sheets for well over a year.

The people of Glasgow were friendly, and there was much to see. I was surprised at the short days. It would get dark about half past three. With the blackout and not being familiar with the city, it was easy to get lost after four in the afternoon.

There were several men from our company who went to Glasgow. We normally ate in the pubs. One pub became the special place for us. It was at the corner of Soccyhall and Renfrew streets. This is where I met Willy Fife, the man who wrote the song "My Heart Belongs to Glasgow, Good Old Glasgow Town." A group of us would sing that and other songs with him. We did the buying, and he always had scotch with a pint of beer. When he finished the scotch, he would let every drop drain into the beer so as not to waste it. I had a quart of USP alcohol with me so we did not have to spend as much money on hard liquor. One time I gave a shot of pure alcohol to an Australian soldier who had been in North Africa with the 8th Army. That got him singing, and he would sing the songs "Walzing Matilda" and "Lily Marlene." I had a good time in Glasgow.

The Salvation Army would always solicit money in the pubs. All soldiers would give to them because, each time we entered the U.K., there would be a Salvation Army person there to give us a little ditty bag with toilet articles. They seemed to know what we needed at the right time.

I also ate at the Scottish version of a five-and-ten store. I had a breakfast of sausage and eggs. The sausages tasted like they were made from sawdust, and the eggs were scrambled powdered eggs. The civilians had a rough time in the United Kingdom during the war. They suffered many bombings, worked long hours and had little choice in food. I did go to one nice restaurant, where I was embarrassed by the antics of one U.S. soldier. This soldier, like everyone else, had waited a long time for service. To show his displeasure, he took out a pack of razor blades and started to chew them up and seemed to swallow the blades. This caused quite a commotion, and eventually he was ejected. I later learned that he had been a circus man in civilian life and this was one of his circus tricks. In all respects, it was a very enjoyable furlough but I was happy to get back to the company.

The Christmas of 1943 was the second one I had away from the States. However, it was in a much better environment than in 1942, where we spent Christmas engaged in a desperate battle at Longstop Hill in Tunisia. I think it was the better living conditions and being in an English-speaking country that made me and all the others feel homesick at this time.

During the Christmas week, we would go to a pub in Weymouth and listen to all the latest songs from the States. Most of them were pertaining to the war, and to us they were quite sad. These songs were "I'll Be Seeing You," "When the Lights Go on Again All over the World," and "I Don't Want to Walk Without You." In particular, the new song "White Christmas" sung by Bing Crosby made everyone homesick. Contributing to our emotions was the uneasiness about the forthcoming battle. We wondered if we would survive the invasion of Europe and ever see home again.

There was also a new musical stage play around, although I did not get an opportunity to see it. The songs from it were popular in England. It was *This Is the Army*, written by Irving Berlin, who was in England with the show. I did get to see Jimmy Cagney perform the songs and dances from *Yankee Doodle Dandy*. He did an excellent job, although he really was out of breath when he finished the dances. I saw the movie in Oran, Algeria, almost a year ago. I also saw a few of the British stage shows, which were good. Their sense of humor was a little different from ours, and some of the jokes were not very funny to us.

January 12–April 24, 1944. Cattistock, Dorset, England

The company left Piddlehinton Barracks at 1000 hours on January 12. We went by motor convoy and traveled 14 miles to Cattistock, Dorset, England. We were the only soldiers in the small village. The barracks were not much to look at. The company was in five small, wooden, one-story buildings. Each one was heated by a stove in the center of the one room. However, it was our new home, and we proceeded to organize the camp. The barracks were in a quaint old British village that had only a few buildings on the main street. There were two pubs in the town. One, called the Three Horseshoes, we occasionally frequented.

The local children were attracted by our camp and would come over to talk to us. They were neat and clean and made a good impression. As a result, they were well-rewarded with gum and candy.

The usual camp duties continued, but now the training was more intense. There were long road marches. Later, they became timed road marches. The goal of the long marches with full field equipment was to attain a rate of five miles per hour. We were told that this might be needed in the next operation.

We also had 36-hour maneuvers that required long marches. The 18th Infantry was training intensively in assault tactics, street fighting, river crossings, reduction of pillboxes and amphibious landings.

On January 16, 1944, the entire 1st Division assembled at a parade ground in Bridport, Dorset, for an inspection by Gen. Montgomery. He was to head the Allied ground forces in the invasion of France. We were all cleaned up, and the entire 1st Division of 15,000 men was standing in a formation of battalions when I heard a commotion in the rear. There was someone barking out an order, "Make way." I turned around, as did all the other men, and saw Gen. Montgomery coming through the ranks from the rear. He was greeting the men rather than inspecting. He was a man of small stature but exuded authority. He spent time talking to some of the men as he went through the division. He then gave a brief speech. It was strange to see a very formal British general, who was known for his reticence, conduct an inspection in this informal way. It could have been because the 1st Division fought side-by-side with Montgomery in North Africa and Sicily, and this was his way of showing respect. It was the strangest inspection I had ever experienced. However, I think it helped to make a stronger bond between the troops of both nations.

During the time we were in Cattistock, there seemed to be more and more troops on intensive maneuvers. I saw the airborne troops practicing with the big gliders, which were pulled by transport planes. They would have two or three gliders on tow lines behind them. The gliders carrying the glider troops would be released when they got close to the target. Then they would land silently near the target. I don't know which is worse, a sea landing on a hostile shore or a glider or parachute landing in a hostile area.

I missed a lot of these maneuvers because I was sent to get more surgical training at an army base hospital in Bristol, England. I spent about a month working there. The work in the operating room was interesting but did not have a direct relation to the work done in an aid station. In an aid station, we did not perform any prepared operations. It was more like an accident ward in a city hospital. We would stop bleeding, administer blood plasma, disinfect wounds, give shots of morphine, immobilize broken bones with splints, tie off ruptured arteries and, in some cases, sew up chest wounds.

However, one incident during an operation reminded me of some of the aid station problems. A soldier had been scheduled to have his appendix removed. I had prepared him for the operation and brought the man into the operating room, where he was anesthetized. The surgeon started by explaining how you determine the place to cut so the appendix would be readily available. He found "Mcburney's point" and made his cut and opened up the man's abdomen. He expected the appendix to be right there and pop out but he couldn't find it. He started to pull out the small intestine, and he must have had it all out because it was all over the table before he found the appendix. At that point, it reminded me of our aid station in combat. It was a big mess. The surgeon finally cut out the appendix and put everything back in and sewed it up. I often wondered how long it took before the man felt normal.

I had been at the hospital a few days when I noticed that one of the x-ray sergeants was a man who had been in the training unit with me at Fitz-simons General Hospital in Denver in 1941. Working at that same hospital was another man who had been in our company in Fort Devens in 1941. It's a small world. I also met one of my old friends, Melvin Duncan, from my home town. He was stationed at an airbase nearby, and I was able to visit him. The air force lived well. They had nice quarters, the best of food and an excellent NCO club.

When I finished my training at the hospital and got back to the company, I found out that I had missed some of the company's extended full-field hikes. Perhaps the time spent working in the hospital was worth it.

During the first week of April, we were "alerted for departure." However, it was not until April 24 that we received orders to "prepare to move to destination unknown".

April 25–29, 1944. Broadmayne, Dorset, England

On April 25, orders came for us to move. It was similar to the way we prepared for the invasion of Sicily. Our company was broken down into smaller units and in the proper sequence to unload in an assault landing.

Three officers and 43 men left Cattistock at 0800 hours and traveled 16 miles by truck to Broadmayne, Dorset, England, arriving at 0915 hours. This was the group I was with and included the entire aid station.

One officer and 16 men left Cattistock at 0800 hours and traveled ten miles by truck to Dorchester, Dorset. They arrived at 0900 hours.

One officer and 19 men left Cattistock at 0800 hours and traveled 14 miles by truck to Piddlehinton, arriving at 1140 hours.

Seven men left Cattistock at 0800 hours and traveled 14 miles by truck to Piddlehinton. They arrived at 1140 hours.

We were all placed in secure areas. This meant we were behind barbed-wire enclosures. We could not leave the area because of security. We were not supposed to talk to anyone about our activities because there could be German spies in the area. The camp was near a P-38 fighter bomber base. I would hear them warming up the engines early each morning, and then they would take off. There must have been a target range nearby because I could hear planes bombing. I believe they were practicing coming in from the ocean and bombing the beaches.

April 30, 1944. Broadmayne, Dorset, England

My group stayed at Broadmayne on the 30th. One officer and 16 men left Dorchester at 2240 hours and traveled 11 miles by truck to the port of Portland. They loaded their ambulances on landing craft LST No. 6 at 0530 hours on May 1. All the other groups stayed in place.

We now knew that this was a maneuver. It was a practice landing, but the security was intense. The food was excellent in the secured camp because special rations had been issued. We were being fattened up for the slaughter.

May 1, 1944. Aboard the landing ship
Dorothea Dix, *Portland harbor*

My group, which consisted of three officers and 43 men, left Broadmayne, Dorset, at 1300 hours and traveled by truck to Weymouth, Dorset. We arrived at 1330 hours and boarded the USS *Dorothea Dix* at 1615 hours.

One officer and 19 men left Piddlehinton at 1300 hours and traveled 15 miles by truck, arriving in Weymouth at 1425 hours. They boarded the USS *Arundel* at 1545 hours.

Seven men left Piddlehinton at 1300 hours and traveled to Portland, arriving at 0900 hours. They loaded their vehicles onto landing craft LST No. 418 at 1600 hours.

May 2–3, 1944. Aboard the Dorothea Dix

We sailed from Portland harbor at 2000 hours on May 3, 1944. We knew this was a maneuver. What we did not know was that the previous group on this maneuver had been attacked by elements of the German navy. I was told by one of the sailors that, on the night of April 27, 1944, three groups of German E-boats (nine torpedo boats) had intercepted the convoy on the way to the landing maneuver site. This happened about ten miles from Portland harbor. The German torpedo boats had sunk two LCIs and had blown the stern off the third one. It suffered casualties but did not sink. We were told that as many as 700 lives were lost that night. This information was kept secret until after the war because it was hoped that the Germans did not know the significance of their attack. It was not known if the Germans had picked up any survivors who might know where and when the invasion of the Continent was to take place.

I was not sure that the sailor had all the facts, and it could have been a rumor. None of this was ever confirmed until the war ended. However, it kept us on edge.

May 4, 1944. Slapton Sands, Devonshire, England

My group transferred to an LCI a few miles from the beach. We used cargo nets as rope ladders to get aboard the smaller boat. The *Dorothea Dix* was a large vessel and carried several thousand men. The LCI carries about 200 men and can get in close to shore. We had traveled on LCIs in the Sicily landing.

This was the English Channel, and the wind was blowing and the water was rough. This made it difficult to climb down the nets because we were loaded down with extra equipment.

I got into the stern compartment, which held about 25–30 men. I soon noticed that one of the men was turning a little white, and sure enough, the rough action of the LCI was making him sick. Someone set a fire pail in front of him, and he threw up in it.

It was starting to get a little warm in the compartment, and I saw others looking at the fire pail and turning pale. Another man got sick and, as he did, he turned his head and threw up into the big ventilating fan. After that, most of the others got sick. I left and went on deck even though it was rough and wet.

We landed at 1800 hours and advanced two miles by foot. Then we set up the aid station near Slapton. At 1800 hours, we advanced another six miles and set up the aid station in the vicinity of Coles Cross, Devonshire. Later, the other groups of our company joined up with us at Coles Cross.

May 5, 1944. Knighton Farm, Devonshire

The entire company left Coles Cross at 1930 hours and traveled to the Knighton Farm area, arriving at 2015 hours.

May 6, 1944. En route to Cattistock, Dorset

Our trucks and ambulances left Knighton Farm for Cattistock, Dorset, at 1515 hours and arrived at 2130 hours. The remainder of the company left Knighton Farm at 2130 hours on quartermaster trucks for Dartmouth and arrived at a dock at 2230 hours. We got on a ferry at 2245 hours to cross the bay for Kingswear. There, we boarded a troop train at 2255 hours. The train left at 2400 hours.

May 7, 1944. Cattistock, Dorset

The train arrived in Maiden Newton at 0435 hours, and we detrained and traveled by truck to Cattistock. We arrived at the barracks at 0455 hours. We all were tired and went to bed.

May 8–15, 1944. Cattistock, Dorset

We were still on the "alert for departure." Duties were to clean up (men, equipment and vehicles). The equipment had to be checked for shortages, and extra medical supplies were issued to carry on the landing.

We had a critique of the maneuver and discussed problems and how to correct them. In general, we thought it went well although most of us who had been on landings before knew that the unexpected always happens on a landing.

May 16–26, 1944. Broadmayne, Dorset

On May 16, my group of five officers and 90 men left Cattistock at 0830 hours by motor convoy en route to area D-9, west of Broadmayne. We arrived at the enclosed, secure area at 0940 hours after traveling 12 miles. Four other men went to Llantarnam, Wales.

On May 25, we were read a letter from the U.S. V Army Corps on the subject of desertion. The main thrust of the letter was that desertion is punishable by death. This was the first time we had ever had this done, and we wondered why now.

Later, we all were issued new assault gas masks, and we all had to try out our gas masks in a test chamber. There seemed to be an emphasis on training for a possible use of poison gas by the Germans. We had not heard any mention of this before. The training was more intense than we had back in the States. Maybe our intelligence group had information about the possible use of poison gas.

All NCOs and officers were briefed on our involvement in the landing in Normandy. We all were given a partial payment of $4.03 in Allied paper money, which was in French francs. I still have the money as there never was a chance to spend it. I cannot figure why it was such an odd sum. There must have been a bookkeeper in charge, and he wanted everything to come out even.

We were given extra men, and 15 enlisted men joined the company on May 25.

May 27, 1944. Broadmayne, Dorset, England

The XAPA No. 1 group of two officers and 41 men prepared to move to area D-12. This was the group I was with. The station platoon was now split into two groups so that in case of severe casualties, one of the groups would survive.

The XAPA No. 2 group of two officers and 30 men prepared to move to area D-5. The LST No. 413 group of one officer and 16 men prepared to move to area D-6. The LST No. 418 group of seven men prepared to move to area D-9. The LCI No. 539 group of four men prepared to join Med. Det. 1st Bn. 18th Infantry. The LCI No. 542 group of four men prepared to join Med. Det. 3d Bn. 18th Infantry. The residue group of 11 men was at the Carlton Hotel, Bournemouth. The Bristol Channel force of three men was at Llantarnam, Wales.

May 28–31, 1944. Broadmayne, Dorset

All the moves were made on the 29th. Briefings on the landing continued. Rations, cigarettes and other field items were issued on May 31. We knew the invasion was on and very soon.

June 1, 1944. Broadmayne, Dorset

It was a beautiful day. We went out on a little grassy hill to review our forthcoming action. The early June sun had warmed up the little knoll and made it comfortable. It was such a nice day that we would have just liked to look at the blue sky and lounge in the sun and read a book. We were still in the sealed area near the port of Portland. We were waiting for orders to board landing craft for the invasion of Europe.

Our company was as well-prepared as possible. We had a full complement of men. We had replacements for those we had lost in North Africa and Sicily. The replacements were new draftees, and they appeared to be excellent men. One man now in my platoon had several years of college and would be a good surgical technician after he got through the initial shock of his first combat experience. He had performed well in the landing maneuvers.

We had just been briefed on our specific job in the landing. Everyone now knew that the 18th Infantry Combat Team would land in Normandy on the second wave on June 5 about 10 A.M. We would land on a beach that was code-named Omaha Easy Red.

We were now sitting around, putting our few belongings in order, and most of the new men were writing letters. Most of the veterans were just talking of past experiences because after almost two years it was hard to write letters.

The new man in my platoon came over to me and started talking. At first, he was just rambling on about his family. Then he went on to say, "I have seen the light. Everything is all right. We have nothing to worry about. God is with us."

He began talking incoherently and every so often would say, "I have seen the light." After a short time, he was shouting and had to be restrained. We quickly got him out of the area and sent him to a hospital. He was our first casualty in the Normandy invasion!

Most of the new men were looking a little scared. This was the first time they had ever seen anyone break down. It must have been difficult for new men with vivid imaginations to hear the veterans describe their experiences. They might believe no one has much of a chance to live through an assault landing. A sensitive person might think he would die within the next few days, and it could be too much for his mind to take. You must put the bad thoughts in the back of your mind and forget them.

I often wondered why some men break down. Perhaps it is the way they are brought up. When my children were young, I tried to instill self-reliance in them so as to protect them from any breakdowns in times of extreme stress.

June 2, 1944. Aboard the Dorothea Dix, *Portland harbor, England*

Our group left area D-12 at 0755 hours, traveled 15 miles by truck to the *Dorothea Dix* and boarded at 1100 hours. The other groups of the company boarded the same day except for the ones coming ashore after D Day.

June 3–4, 1944. Aboard the Dorothea Dix, *Portland harbor*

The landing in France had been set for June 5, but the weather was so bad that it was postponed. We thought we might have to leave the ship and go back to the camps because the weather was so bad. However, it was decided by Gen. Eisenhower to go ahead on June 6.

Twelve

Omaha Beach

June 5, 1944. Aboard the Dorothea Dix *at sea*

The *Dorothea Dix* left Portland harbor, Portland, Dorset, England, at 1645 hours en route to Omaha Easy Red beach in Normandy, France. As we left the harbor, the effect of the bad storm became apparent because the ship started to dip and roll. I knew many men would probably get seasick and hoped it would not affect our performance in the landing.

More ships joined us as we sailed toward France and formed into a long convoy. I could see this was a massive operation. There were LCIs, LSTs and many larger troop ships like ours. A protecting screen of destroyers formed up on the flanks of the convoy. Mine sweepers were clearing a path ahead of the fleet. The large warships (battleships and cruisers) were off in the distance. The weather was overcast, and as we traveled the 100 miles across the channel to the French coast, there was no sign of the Germans either in the air or on the sea.

It was monotonous on the ship because everyone was a bit nervous about tomorrow's action and could not concentrate on a game or a book. The monotony was broken up when we found we had a celebrity aboard. Ernest Hemingway was going over to France on our vessel. I am not sure he planned to land on D Day, but he probably could get a good story about the landing from the Navy people. Perhaps he could even interview some of the wounded when they returned to the ship.

He held a lengthy bull session on the main deck. He was sharp-looking and stood out from the rest of us with his black beard and khaki safari jacket. He really looked like a war correspondent. He liked the attention he was getting from all the soldiers, and he did most of the talking. It was good to have a diversion because, for a while, we could forget what would happen tomorrow.

It was obvious that the Germans did not suspect we would land during such bad weather. We were fearful of what would happen when the Germans finally found out the invasion was on. We expected that most of the German air force would be in action against the fleet. The planners of the invasion must have expected this because many of the ships had large barrage balloons (little blimps) attached to them like a balloon tied to a bicycle. They were supposed to prevent low-level bombing and strafing by the enemy.

The plan of attack was to have the British force land on our left at beaches called Juno and Gold. On our right, the U.S. 4th Division would land on a beach called Utah. The 1st Infantry Division, along with a regiment of the 29th Infantry Division, which was attached to the 1st Division, would land in the center at the beach called Omaha. The 16th and 116th Infantry Regimental Combat Teams would be the first units to land on Omaha. With them would be the engineers, who would blow up the beach obstacles and bulldoze exits from the beach.

Sunrise was about 0600 hours on June 6, and low tide was about 0530 hours. H hour, the time the initial units were to hit the beach, was set at 0630 hours, or about one hour after low tide.

The 18th Infantry Combat Team would land in the second wave. This was scheduled for 0930. We were part of this group. After securing the beach, the units were to drive inland and make contact with the units on each side to consolidate the beachhead. On the night of June 5-6, paratroopers of the 82d and 101st Airborne Divisions were supposed to land inland, secure strategic points and make contact with the seaborne troops.

During the night, we heard the planes going over for hours. These were probably the paratroopers or bombers bombing the beaches. We hoped the bombing of the beach defenses would make it easier for the seaborne troops to land. We later found that the beaches never were bombed because of poor visibility.

Our group was to land on the section of Omaha beach called Easy Red. The aid station platoon was split up into two groups so, in case one group did not make it, there would be one left. The other group was on the troop transport USS *Joseph Thurston.*

June 6, 1944. Colleville-sur-Mer (1½ miles northwest), Normandy, France

We were awake before dawn, and after a quick breakfast, got ready to wait for our turn to load onto a smaller craft for the landing on the beach. The troop transports were anchored about ten miles from shore. There was a recorded speech by Gen. Eisenhower over the ship's loudspeaker, wishing us luck. This did not have much effect on us because we were thinking of the landing and what we might encounter onshore. The weather was still bad. It was misty and overcast.

The visibility at first was poor, but it gradually improved to about ten miles. The wind was strong, and the waves were about three to four feet high where we were on the large troop transports. It probably would be higher near the beaches. This would make it difficult for us unless the smaller landing craft could get in very close to the shore.

I could hear the big guns on the warships firing as well as the guns on the shore. I knew that not all the gunfire ashore was ours because we had delays in troops moving off our ship. We were told that many of the smaller landing boats had been sunk by German artillery. There was a great deal of smoke coming from the beach, but I could not really see what was going on.

I had a camera with me and had it slung high around my neck so it would not get wet. However, it was very visible and was noticed by a CIC (counterintelligence) officer who took it from me. He said he would return it later. Which he did. I never could understand why he did this, for I am sure the pictures would have been invaluable in any critique of the landing. There were very few pictures taken on Omaha beach that day.

We had been waiting on the troop ship *Dorothea Dix* for several hours when we heard the small landing craft we were supposed to go on had been sunk. We had to be rescheduled on a different landing craft. The wait was hard to take because we were all at a high pitch of excitement. It was a feeling between dread and the desire to get going, and any delay increased the dread. At last, we were told we were next to go ashore. A large tank lighter was brought alongside the *Dorothea Dix*. This was a flat-bottomed vessel that did not ride well in rough seas. It was not normally used to carry soldiers, but so many of the smaller landing craft had been sunk that this was all they had.

We climbed over the rail and down the side, using the rope cargo nets as ladders, and stepped into the bouncing landing craft. You had to be very careful not to fall between the large ship and the smaller landing craft because of the uneven pitching of the two vessels. Finally we were all boarded except one man, who fell overboard and was caught between the two vessels. He was pulled out and did not seem to be badly hurt. He was the object of envy for he would miss the landing. We had several hundred men in the landing craft. This included a U.S. Navy shore party, which was going ashore to direct naval gunfire.

When we were pulling away from the transport, one of the naval officers pointed to several battleships and said, "That is the *Nevada*. It was sunk by the Japanese at Pearl Harbor. It was salvaged to fight here. The *Nevada* has 12-inch guns, and the other battleship is the *Texas* with 14-inch guns. They should be able to outrange anything the Germans have."

Our landing boat had to circle for quite a while because there were many landing boats ready to go ashore, but only a few holes had been blown through the beach obstacles. We had to wait for our turn.

Off to one side, there was a barge about a half mile from the beach with four cranes sticking up like four giraffes. As I watched, a shell hit the barge on one end, and it slowly started to list and sink, with one side going down first. The cranes fell into the ocean like little toys. Finally, they all disappeared under the water.

As we proceeded toward shore, I could see some LCIs and smaller craft burning on the beach. As we got closer, I could see German shell fire hitting the beach. I also could see that there were many beach obstacles still in place. These beach obstacles were mined metal triangles that would rip the bottom out of the boats and then set off powerful explosives to blow up the landing craft. This meant the engineers were having trouble, and we had only a few places to come ashore. We knew that, beyond the beach, there would be barbed wire, concertina wire, anti-tank ditches, machine gun emplacements and land mines to further hinder any advance inland. Nearby, there were two destroyers, very close to shore, just drifting and firing their guns point-blank at the pillboxes on the hill above the beach. The battleships were farther out and were firing the big guns overhead, and we could hear and feel the blast of the guns.

At last, we got clearance to land, and the landing craft started in toward shore at full speed. Our group of about 20 men moved up toward the front of the landing craft. Most of us had been on assault landings before, and we wanted to be able to get off before the German artillery ranged in on the tank lighter. But we did not want to be the first ones off in case there was small arms fire hitting the ramp, so we positioned ourselves about five or six rows behind the lead men.

The landing craft grounded on a sandbar in about two feet of water. We ran down the ramp and waded to shore, picking our way through the obstacles. There did not seem to be any small arms fire on this part of the beach.

The German artillery fire was not very heavy. The shells were landing up and down the beach in a somewhat predictable manner, so we could gauge when to run and when to dive to the ground. We ran as fast as possible over the hard-packed sand and went inland for about 20 feet to an area of shingle. This consisted of smooth semi-flat stones about two to three inches in diameter. The shingle led farther inland to the ravine, or draw, we were supposed to use in exiting Omaha beach. The stones were slippery and hard to run on.

I went on until I came to where about 20–30 infantrymen were lying at the approach to the draw. I yelled to them to see why they were not moving out. There was no response, and none of them moved. I crawled over to the nearest man to see what the problem was. I found that he was dead, and so were all the others. There was a German machine gun nest at the mouth of the draw, and they had all been caught in the fire as they tried to leave the beach. I immediately scuttled on my hands and legs off to the right, where there was some protection from a small hill of sand. When I say scuttled, I mean moving like a crab with no space between you and the ground and going fast. We had to decide what to do next.

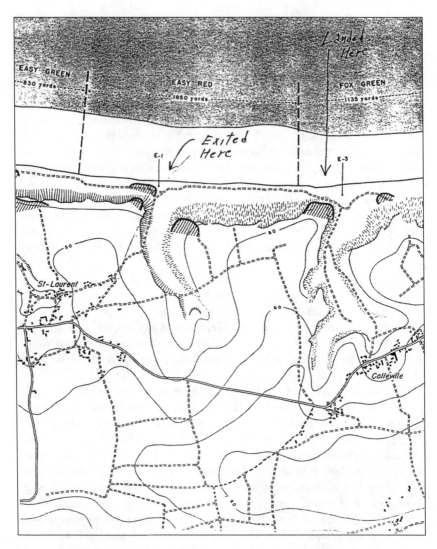

Our landing and exiting areas on Omaha beach on June 6, 1944. The map comes from *Omaha Beachhead*, a publication of the Historical Division of the War Dept.

I was scared, and my mouth got so dry I could hardly talk. Sgt. Woods, who was next to me, leaned over and asked what was wrong. I croaked back, "My mouth is so dry, I can't swallow never mind talk."

After a short time, I calmed down and took a good look at the situation. There was no small arms fire on this section of the beach. While there were many German shells landing on the beach, they seemed to be random fire from mortars and artillery. However, the Germans still had some view of the area because the landing boats were having shells land near them, and occasionally one would be hit.

There were not many soldiers in the immediate area. Except for the landing boat that dropped us off, no other boat came in at this part of the beach. Were we in the right location? We soon decided that the Navy had brought us in far to the left (east) of the proper landing spot, and we had tried to leave the beach through draw E-3. This is where the dead infantrymen were. We were supposed to leave the beach at draw E-1, about a mile to our right (west). I found out later that draw E-3 had not been secured and was still in German hands. It was a good thing we did not try to leave the beach via draw E-3 because we would have run into the same German machine gun fire.

So, after being so scared, I got a little angry and decided to do something useful. I had learned a long time back that if you are really scared, the best way to keep your fear in the background is to get angry and keep busy.

Our group, of about 20 men, moved west (to our right as we faced inland), all the time running and diving to the ground as the shells came in near us. We ran along the beach toward draw E-1 until we came to a beach aid station. Here, the Navy had set up a collection point where the wounded were being collected so they could be brought back aboard the ships.

At this part of Easy Red beach, the sand portion was about 100 yards wide with areas of swamp along the inland edge of the flat. The bluff overlooking the beach was about 125 feet high and was reached by 200 yards of moderate slope, which had patches of heavy brush. We were supposed to meet the other half of our group near here and leave the beach and go inland. First, we had to find out where they were.

We used the aid station as our meeting place, and while several men went looking for the other group, the rest of us went up and down the beach, picking up and helping the wounded men and bringing them to the beach aid station. The beach was still under shell fire, and many of the wounded men were staying in place because they did not know where to go. Others were in a partial state of shock and needed help to the aid station.

There was wreckage all along the beach. There were tanks, trucks and all kinds of gear. I went by one landing boat that had dropped its ramp right in front of another exit, and the Germans had opened fire as the soldiers left the boat. Many of them had been hit and killed as they tried to run down the ramp. All of the wounded had been removed, but the dead were still sprawled in front of the vessel. The landing craft was disabled and burning, half out of the water. The beach was a shambles. I saw a tank that had come in at low tide underneath a disabled landing craft that had come in at a higher tide.

There were supposed to be 64 amphibious tanks ashore to help the infantry but, because of the rough seas, only 29 were launched, and of these, 27 swamped and sank. Only two got ashore.

One of the unusual things I saw on the beach was a yellow Piper Cub airplane. They were used by artillery spotters. The plane seemed to be in perfect shape, as if it had come over from England and landed there. About a half hour later, I saw it get hit by a shell and go up in flames. I found out later that a flight of these planes had flown over from England to help the Navy direct the gunfire. The fleet had been told not to fire on them but, in a battle, everyone fires on anything strange. They all were shot down by our own Navy.

After a while, we made contact with our other aid station group and proceeded to leave the beach. We crossed the anti-tank ditch and another ditch that was flooded. We then went up the hill through the German minefield. There was a path through the minefield. It had been made by the first infantrymen. Some of the leading men had tripped the mines and several men, who were not badly wounded, remained there to guide the rest of us through the minefield. They were stationed along the cleared route. One of them had his foot blown off at the ankle. He had been bandaged up and was quite cheerful. He probably figured it was safer on the side of the hill than on the beach. He knew the war was over for him. A lot of the men were envious of him.

We finally got up onto the bluff overlooking the beach. By now, the 16th and 18th Infantry had infiltrated behind the Germans. They had knocked out the machine gun nests and other strong points the enemy was using to protect draw E-1. This portion of the beach was now secure from German small arms fire.

We dug our slit trenches and set up our temporary aid station on the beach side of the hill so the German shells would go over our heads. We started to evacuate the casualties to the beach. From where we were, we had a good view of the beach. The engineers had cleared out several openings through the beach obstacles and were now bulldozing a road up the draw. Vehicles were starting to leave the beach area.

Enemy shells were still landing on the beach, and there was a tremendous amount of wreckage on the beach. Some of the larger landing boats were still burning as more troops and vehicles were coming ashore and going inland. The battleship and cruisers were now firing at points inland. The blast from the battleships guns could be felt where we were, and we could see the incandescent shells going overhead. The targets were so far away we never heard the shells land.

Later that night, some German aircraft flew over the beachhead, but there was no problem because a fleet of 4,000 vessels can throw up a lot of flak. A few German planes were shot down.

Our two groups that landed, totaling four officers and 70 men, had a few casualties: Pvt. Herald E. Vose (shell fragment, left leg), Pvt. Clifford G. Carton (severe burns, head and left side), Pvt. John Mancino (burns, head and hands), Pvt. Robert Winchester (shell fragment, right buttocks), Pvt. Joseph T. Chiofole (burns, left forehead; remained on duty), and Pvt. Real L. LaGasse (burns, both hands; remained on duty). All the burns occurred when a German shell hit a truck carrying gasoline and ammunition.

Two other men were reported missing in action: Pvt. Ezra K. Waldrop, and Pvt. Albert Zimmerman.

The seven men who were with an 18th Infantry unit landed safely. All our vehicles that were supposed to land were still on ships offshore as the congestion on the beach was immense.

The penetration on the first day on Omaha beach was about 1½ miles, and the entire beachhead was still under enemy mortar and artillery fire.

June 7, 1944. Colleville-sur-Mer, Normandy, France

At dawn, the fleet moved in closer, and it was hard to imagine the enormous group of vessels. There were troop ships, all sizes of merchant ships, LSTs, huge barges and all types of naval vessels. It looked as if all the ships

Temporary Aid Station in Normandy, France, on June 7, 1944. *Left to right:* Sgt. Towne, Pvt. Jones, Sgt. McFarland, and Lt. Gaumari.

in the world were here. If Hitler had seen this, he would have sued for peace. There was no German air activity, and the trucks, tanks and men were coming ashore continually. We moved, on foot, from our position overlooking the beach to a position about 2 miles inland. We dug in and set up a temporary aid station. We had only the medical supplies we carried ashore.

At 1300 hours, LST No. 413 landed. It carried one officer and 16 men with six ambulances and two jeeps. They managed to get to the aid station at 1700 hours. A skeleton aid station was set up, and ambulances were sent to the 18th Infantry Battalions. We then proceeded to evacuate casualties to the beach, where the clearing company of the 1st Medical Battalion was now set up.

There was no enemy activity in the immediate area. We now were evacuating not only the 18th Combat Team casualties and German wounded, but we had some French civilians who had been hurt in the recent action.

Two of the civilian wounded stand out. They came in late at night. One was a French woman, who had a shell fragment hit her in one arm, which caused a severe compound fracture. Her arm was so badly damaged we could not immobilize it properly. The muscles had pulled the broken bone in the upper arm up beyond the break and made the arm look about six inches shorter. We did not have any traction splints ashore, so we did the best we could, gave her a shot of morphine and sent her to the clearing company.

We also had an older man who had a large potbelly. He had a shell or bomb fragment rip open the skin on his belly area and expose all his intestines. Again, we had a difficult time with this. It did not look as if any of the intestines were damaged so all we could do was to cover them, tie them in and send him back where they could operate. They both would be sent to England.

The landing at Omaha beach had been more difficult than had been expected. Unknown to Allied intelligence, in addition to the 726th German Infantry Division manning the beach emplacements, the 352d German Infantry Division (a first-class field division) was engaged in anti-invasion maneuvers immediately behind the assault beach at the time of our landing.

Thus, the Germans had a great initial advantage in manpower at Omaha beach. However, the 1st Division had been able to defeat an entire enemy field division, which had been well-entrenched in prepared positions, and had driven the enemy back. The Germans in this area never recovered from this because they did not have any other reserves to counterattack.

Gen. Bradley later made a comment about Omaha beach and the 1st Division's performance:

> Had a less experienced division than the First Infantry Division stumbled onto this crack resistance, it might easily have been thrown back into the Channel. Unjust though it was, it was my choice of the 1st to spearhead the invasion that probably saved us Omaha Beach and a catastrophe on the landing.*

*A Soldier's Story (1957), page 272.

The 1st Division, famous for its night attacks, made another on this night and, by the end of the 7th of June, had occupied Huppain. We were now close to a juncture with the British on our left near Port-en-Bessin.

Units of the 18th Infantry Combat Team crossed the Bayeux-Isigny highway and occupied the high ground that dominated the approaches to the Aure river and crossed the Aure river in several places. In Bellefontaine, the 18th captured a bridge intact and got some tanks across. Mosles was also captured.

June 8, 1944. Surrain, Normandy, France

We moved from the last location 2½ miles on foot. We dug in and set up the station and proceeded to evacuate casualties. More vehicles arrived from LST No. 418 and joined the company at 1600 hours. This group of vehicles consisted of a 1¾–ton truck, a water trailer and two more ambulances.

The 18th Infantry again attacked at midnight and occupied Formigny. Other units of the 1st Division took Tour-en-Bessin that evening. We had been evacuating many German casualties as well as our own in the past couple of days.

June 9, 1944. Mosles, Normandy, France

We moved from the last station by foot two miles to the new location. We dug in and set up the aid station. Evacuation proceeded, including Germans and civilians.

By the morning of June 9, the 1st Division had reached all of its D-Day objectives. The division had taken over 600 prisoners and killed many others in this action. The division renewed its attack on the 9th and advanced all night. Naval gunfire was still being used very effectively even though the division was over six miles inland.

June 10, 1944. Le Tronquay, Normandy, France

We moved from the last area to the new location by truck (eight miles). We dug in and set up the aid station. We were now over 12 miles inland, and the division held the dominant terrain in the Cerisy forest.

The next objective of the division was Caumont. This was a road junction of importance. Caumont lies on a hill mass more than 750 feet above sea level and is forward of the Cerisy forest and would give our artillery control of the upper Drome valley. Its capture would make the hold on the beachhead secure and serve as a base for further offensive action into the hilly country to the south. Possession of Caumont would threaten the enemy's lateral communications from Caen to the St. Lo-Vire-Avrances region.

June 11, 1944. Balleroy (½ mile south), France

We moved eight miles from our last area by truck. We were now about 12 miles from Omaha Beach. We dug in and set up the aid station and continued to evacuate the wounded. We knew another attack was to start soon, and the combat team was waiting for other units to protect the flanks. The 1st Division was now farther inland than any other Allied unit. The British, who were supposed to be on our immediate left flank, had not been able to keep up, and there were no U.S. Army units on our right flank.

Early in the morning, a French civilian came into the aid station. In my broken French, I asked him what he wanted. He said he was with the FFI (the French Underground) and handed me an envelope. I noticed it was a British Service envelope. I opened the folded note that was inside. In English was the following message:

> Please bring help
> We are at La Bazoque. There are two British commandos and one British sailor We are all wounded one has his right foot cut off.
> Please hurry we have been like this for 5 days. You can bring back one stretcher
> Are two here
> Please hurry
> Thon A.I. Goog, K.R. Morris RN, G. Hargreaves. RM

The French resistance fighters had found them and taken them to a safe place. Because our division had advanced farther than any other Allied unit, the French resistance man asked us to take care of the wounded men. He said he would guide us. I asked him if there were any Germans in the area. He said he had not seen soldiers when he was on his way to our aid station and did not know where the Germans were. Neither did I.

I got one of the ambulances and, with Cpl. Mike Katchur driving and the Frenchman on the running board, we left the aid station. We went off in a southwesterly direction. This was a different direction than the 18th Infantry's advance toward the next objective. The 18th Infantry was on the right flank of the division, so we were proceeding into unknown territory.

We were traveling along a small, narrow road with tall hedgerows on each side. The hedgerows were like high fences, and we had no idea what was behind them and could not see if there were any German units in the area.

This worried me, and I hoped we did not meet up with any German patrols or drive into an ambush.

We were not going fast, and it seemed like we had been driving for a long time when we came to a dirt driveway that led to a small barn. The Frenchman motioned for us to go up to the barn. When we got there, he jumped off and opened the barn door. There were the three British servicemen, and they were glad to see us. They had been given good treatment by the FFI and did not need any immediate attention so we quickly loaded them into the ambulance.

We left our guide there and retraced the route back to the aid station. At our aid station we redressed their wounds and, after giving them hot drinks and food, we sent them back to our clearing company.

We saw no one on the trip, which was about 3½ miles each way, and there was no sign that any soldiers had ever been there. The Germans must have left, and none of the U.S. Army units had filled the gap. I believe the U.S. 2d Infantry Division was supposed to be there. It is amazing that sometimes, in an important battle, you can drive for miles in areas between the opposing forces and not see any soldiers.

June 12, 1944. Cormolain, France

After a three-mile move, our company set up in the small Normandy village of Cormolain. We were on the main road and located in an apple orchard close to the center of town. We could see the steeple of the local church and hear the church bell, which rang several times a day. The aid station was set up in a tent because we had been receiving a lot of the casualties at night. We needed a place where we could work after dark. In the blacked-out tent, we could use our Colman lanterns and really see what we were doing when we worked on the wounded.

Everyone dug in because enemy artillery was very active. Evacuation was proceeding and, at first, the enemy offensive activity was light. We were well within the range of German artillery and mortar fire so we dug deep holes. Because we were in a wooded area, we put boards and logs on top of the holes and covered them with sandbags and dirt. We did this because, if a shell exploded on a limb of a nearby tree, we would be protected from the shell fragments.

On the 12th, the division started another attack at night and, after house-to-house fighting, Caumont was captured. This was the high ground in the area and gave our artillery observers excellent observation into the enemy positions.

Things were quiet for about a week, with only occasional shelling by the Germans. During this period, the children from the village would come over

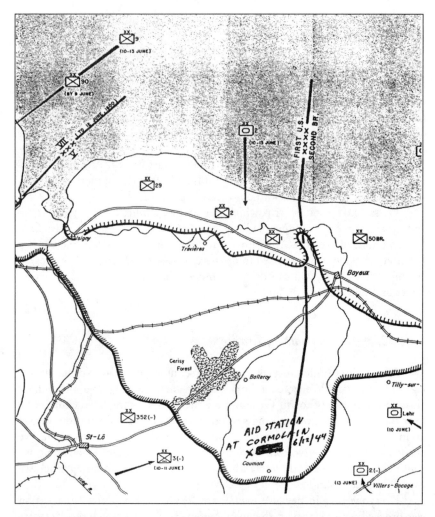

Position of the Aid Station at Cormolain, Normandy on June 12, 1944. The map comes from the *Omaha Beachhead*, a publication of the Historical Division of the War Dept.

and watch us hold sick call and treat the few men wounded by German artillery fire or from patrol activity.

The regimental dentist had set up his equipment in our aid station, and the local children were fascinated with the compact dental chair and the foot-powered drill. When it was not in use, one of them would sit in the chair and another would pretend to drill his teeth. It was amazing to us how the young French children could all speak English. We gave them candy and gum. They, in turn, invited us to their homes, where their parents would give us fresh

Sgt. McFarland in his sleeping quarters in Cormolain, Normandy.

bread, wine and Calvados. Calvados was made from apples, and I first thought it was cider. I soon found out, after taking a big swallow, that it was much stronger. It must have been distilled hard cider because it seemed to be almost pure alcohol. Some of the men used it in their cigarette lighters. The French mix it with water before drinking it.

After about a week, the Germans started to move more troops into the area. They were massing elements of the German 3d Parachute Division and the 2d Panzer Division around us. The shelling of our area became more frequent, and we had an increase in combat casualties. Many of our men complained that the church steeple must have a German spotter in it and wanted it shot down. But, as it was inside our lines, it was unlikely any German spotter was using it, so it remained intact. We did, however, put more dirt on our covered holes, and most men slept in them at night. Some of the men used the hedgerows as part of their foxholes. These were the high earthen boundaries to the fields in Normandy.

During the periods of rather intense shelling, we had problems with some of our men, who would not stay in one place. They would be in one covered hole and then think another hole was safer and would keep running around. These men had to be restrained until they quieted down or they might get hit. Most of the time, this would be a problem with the new men, but sometimes the strain would build up and some of the veterans were affected.

An Aid Station in Cormolain, Normandy. *Top:* Two French boys are playing dentist and patient. *Bottom (left to right):* unknown soldier, French girl, Cpl. Carney, Pvt. Miller.

June 13–July 7, 1944. Cormolain, France

By June 13, 1944 the 1st Infantry Division had advanced 20 miles inland from Omaha beach. The 18th Infantry Combat Team was in the French town of Caumont, along with other 1st Division units. The British 50th Division on our left and the U.S. 2d Infantry Division on our right had only advanced about eight miles leaving us way out in a salient. We had German army units in front and on both flanks. It was not a desirable situation, so the division was told to dig in and hold defensive positions until the other units could come abreast of us.

The aid station was in operation all this time, but we did not have many casualties because, except for patrols, the 18th Infantry was waiting for the other units to come abreast. This never happened.

The 18th Infantry Regiment was awarded a presidential citation for outstanding performance during the ten days following the D-Day landing on the coast of Normandy.

One day, we had a visit from Father McEvoy, the regimental chaplain. He used to stay with our aid station during the North African and Sicilian campaigns. I had heard that he had been sick, and I was amazed that he did not recognize me or the others in the aid station. It is possible that he had seen so many of the men he had known for years come through badly wounded or die in our aid station that he could not bear to talk to us.

We had five replacements join the company on June 15 and 12 more on June 18. They would take the place of the men lost in the landing. Our residue group in England left Southampton on an LST at 2000 hours on June 14 and joined the company at 1700 hours on the 15th.

By June 14, facing the 1st Division in a half circle were elements of the German 5th Parachute Regiment, the 3d German Parachute Division and the 38th Panzer Eng. Bn. of the 2d Panzer Division.

On the 15, the Germans shelled Caumont almost continually and launched a counterattack against the 18th Infantry. They did not gain any ground and lost heavily to our artillery and mortar fire.

One reason for the slowdown in the American offensive that contributed to the lack of success of the other units to come abreast of us was the fierce storm that arose on June 18, which lasted for four days. This storm destroyed the floating docks that had been towed over from England. Because of this, there was a problem getting enough ammunition for a period of time. This gave the Germans time to bring up more troops and prepare defenses.

We had a lot of interruptions because of the Germans shelling our area. The infantrymen who would come in for sick call said they felt safer in their own location. Of course, they had their own covered holes there.

On the night of June 25, the Germans became very active with mortar fire. They were so close that we could hear the mortars go off with a pop and then hear them crash as they landed. Later, a German tank started firing into our area, and this time I went to my hole. You can tell when a tank is firing because you hear the crack of it shooting and then almost immediately hear the noise of the exploding shell. The shelling continued, and I felt somewhat safe in my hole although you always wonder if you might get a direct hit. You cannot keep from shivering everytime the tank fires.

After about 20 minutes of shelling, I heard some men screaming. Someone must have been hit! The screams seemed to be coming from the area about 200-300 yards away, where an anti-aircraft gun had recently been set up. This anti-aircraft unit had large 90-mm guns which could also be used as artillery or as antitank defense. They were similar to the well-respected German 88-mm guns.

It was quite dark, and the tank was still shelling, and no one wanted to leave their covered holes. I reluctantly got out of my hole, and with some difficulty, persuaded about 20 men to get litters and come with me. We had to cross a field and go down and up a ravine and then we entered a wooded area. All the time, the German tank was still firing into the area. As we came close to the source of the screams, we had to use our flashlights and felt very exposed. We finally found the wounded men near the anti-aircraft gun. The crew had an uncovered hole under a tree. It must have been their first action because you never have an open hole under a tree in areas that are under enemy shell fire.

There were five men in the open hole. A German shell had hit the tree and burst, spraying all five of them with steel splinters. I checked them over for bleeding and could not find any wounds that required immediate attention. However, they seemed to be in a great deal of pain. We put them on litters so we could carry them back to the aid station. There we had a gasoline lantern in the blacked out tent and we could really examine the wounded men. The tank was still firing so, even though it was a hard carry, we got back quickly.

After we got the wounded men in the tent, the litter bearers ran back to their holes. Our two doctors checked the wounded men and could not find any bad wounds. They were perplexed as to what was wrong. The wounded men were very angry and expected us to do something so the doctors decided to give them plasma. We were just starting to give them blood plasma when, one by one, all five men died. The doctors speculated that the men had so many steel splinters in them that they were all cut up inside and had bled to death internally.

I was shocked by the death of five men who did not seem to have any bad wounds. I was also surprised by the reactions of these wounded men. Never before had I encountered wounded soldiers who were angry at the men who had picked them up and were trying to help them. Perhaps it was because they were new to combat and never expected to get hurt. On the other hand, we were used to taking care of men who not only expected to get wounded but wondered if they would ever survive the war. By now, most of us had ceased to hope that we would ever get back to the States. This attitude of resignation to being hit or killed must change your reaction to being wounded. I had talked to many wounded men who were relieved to have been wounded. They would say, "Maybe the war is over for me."

We all went back to our holes and sent the bodies back to the graves registration unit in the morning when things were quieter. I slept in the aid station tent most of the time so that someone would always be available. One time, a soldier was brought in the aid station who, upon initial examination, was dead. However, we could not see any good reason as to why he should have died. We decided to keep the body until daylight because having an ambulance carrying a dead body a considerable distance at night in a blackout is not worth it. After a short time (I was already asleep), Capt. Merriman, the company commander, woke me and said, "Let's try something."

I got a long hypodermic needle and sterilized it. Capt. Merriman filled the syringe with a strong stimulant. He then plunged the needle directly into the man's heart. The man's heart began to beat. We then gave him plasma and sent him back to a field hospital. The next day, we went to the field hospital to check on his condition. He was still alive but was in a coma. I often wondered if he ever fully recovered.

July 8–13, 1944. Planquery, France

We moved, by truck, from Cormolain about 1½ miles to another small town, named Planquery. This new area would not be under as much shell fire and should be quieter. We dug in, and the aid station was set up. Evacuation was proceeding as usual.

We had heard that some units on the beachhead had been attacked by American fighter planes. Some men thought that the Germans were either using captured aircraft or had modified some of theirs to look like our planes. Because of this, when a group of four planes that looked like U.S. P-47s came over and started strafing our positions, the anti-aircraft halftracks opened fire on them. These halftracks have four 50-caliber machine guns mounted close together on a mobile turret, so the gunner has a quick response. Because all four machine guns fire at the same time, they are a devastating weapon. They can blow a plane to pieces.

The planes were coming down one after another, all the time firing their machine guns at us. We all dived into our holes and let the anti-aircraft people take care of the planes. They did quite a job. The first plane caught the full force of the guns and was practically blown to pieces and crashed nearby. The pilot never had a chance. The second plane was hit at a higher altitude,

The wheel of a P-47 our anti-aircraft group shot down in Normandy. It just missed Sgt. Woods. *Left to right:* Sgt. McFarland, Sgt. Woods, Sgt. Sherman, Cpl. Damron.

and the pilot managed to eject from the plane but he was so low that his parachute did not open. The plane crashed and exploded nearby. The pilot hit the ground and bounced in the air. The third plane was also hit, and the pilot ejected. Since he was higher, his parachute opened, and he drifted down a distance away. The fourth plane was even higher, and he managed to pull out of the dive and get away with no apparent damage.

In a few minutes, after things had settled down, I got an ambulance and went over to where the pilot had hit the ground to see if there was any possibility that he was alive. When I got there, the pilot was lying on the ground, and he looked like a broken rag doll. Most of his bones were broken and sticking out (compound fractures). I examined him and could see he was not breathing. I checked his pulse and could not feel any. He must have been killed instantly. He did not have any bullet wounds so it was the impact of hitting the ground that killed him. I checked his dog tags and determined he was an American pilot, only 21 years old. I also noticed that he was not wearing boots. One of the infantrymen saw me looking at the pilot's feet and came over and said, "The pilot had a nice pair of new boots that looked like they were my size. Mine were worn out, so I figured he wouldn't need his anymore."

He showed me the shiny new boots he had already put on. "They sure are a perfect fit."

I had to agree with him. The pilot of the third plane, whose parachute opened, landed safely and was unhurt. None of the soldiers on the ground were hurt by the strafing. The attack by the U.S. planes was a costly mistake because two pilots were killed and three planes were lost.

When I got back to the aid station to unload the body, Sgt. Woods came into the aid station, rolling a wheel assembly of a plane. He had been at the slit trench latrine when the planes came over. When he looked up, he saw a large object coming down near him. He thought it was a bomb, and he was a goner. However, it did not explode because it was the wheel of the first plane, blown off by the anti-aircraft fire.

Later in the day, we were notified that Pvt. Ezra K. Waldrop was removed from the "missing in action" list as of June 6, 1944, to seriously wounded in action with a shell fragment wound in the head and white phosphorus burns on the left shoulder, arm and side of the leg.

Thirteen

Breakout

July 14–19, 1944. Bricqueville-sur-Mer, France

On July 14, the 18th Infantry Combat Team was relieved by units of the 5th U.S. Infantry Division. They took over our positions in the Caumont area. Our company left Planquery on July 14 at 1345 hours and traveled by truck 13½ miles northeast to Bricqueville-sur-Mer. The area was not in an active zone, so we could relax for the first time since the 6th of June. We were able to take showers and obtain clean clothes. We also cleaned and repaired all the equipment and vehicles. It was a welcome relief to be out of the range of German shell fire, and we did not have to sleep in holes. We could rest, and we even saw an old movie.

I figured that we were not taken out of the lines just for a rest and guessed that we were preparing for another big attack. It seems that whenever we are withdrawn from the line, we always end up in a violent battle. However, we all realized that the Allied armies had to break through the German lines soon before the Germans moved in so many reinforcements that a breakout would be very difficult and costly.

On July 19, we got orders to prepare to leave.

July 20–24, 1944. Haut Verney, France

We left the bivouac area at Bricqueville on July 20 at 0125 hours and traveled by truck 18 miles southwest to the new area and arrived at 0430. The roads were good, and the weather misty.

On July 24, Pvt. Albert Zimmerman's status was changed from MIA (missing in action) as of June 6, 1944, to KIA (killed in action) as of June 6, 1944. We have had many of our men wounded, but Pvt. Zimmerman was the first one in our company killed. He was a new replacement, and I did not know him very well. It seems that the new men become casualties more often than the veterans.

The litter bearers and three ambulances were sent to the 18th Infantry

Battalion. This meant that an attack was imminent. We never send our men to the battalions unless they expect a lot of casualties.

The entire 1st Infantry Division was now in an assembly area, ready to move on the attack to break out of the beachhead. We were massed behind the 9th Infantry Division. The 9th had the task of pushing through the German lines after a huge U.S. air bombardment. Then, the 1st Division and part of the 3d Armored Division, attached to the 1st Division for this operation, was to attack through this gap and get behind the German forces. The division would hold the gap open and let our armored divisions sweep through.

The attack was delayed because of bad weather. Our bombers needed good visibility because they were planning to bomb the German troops directly in front of our lines. This required great accuracy so as not to hit our own men. It was to be a massive saturation bombing to soften up the Germans and make it easy for the 9th Division to break through their defenses.

We were now in an attractive wooded area (called Les Bois de Losque) and did not mind the wait. It was a pleasant place, and we were shaded from the sun by the leaves of the young trees. The weather was warm, and we were not under shell fire.

July 25–26, 1944. Les Champs de Losque, France

We had front-row seats to observe the largest saturation bombing ever made on enemy troops. We were still at Haut Verney. The bombing runs started at about 1100 hours on July 25. The weather was clear, and the pilots had good visibility. The air attack commenced with 350 fighter bombers coming low over the German positions. We could see our planes swooping down over the German lines strafing and dropping their bombs. Then came 1,500 heavy bombers (B-17s and Liberators), each carrying 40 100-pound bombs. Flight after flight came over with a tremendous roar, and the bombs were falling close ahead of us. The ground was trembling, and the trees were shaking with the shock. It seemed as if the bombs were landing nearer and nearer. After the heavy bombers, 350 more fighter bombers came over to strafe and bomb again. Finally, as if this was not enough, our artillery started, with about 1, 000 big guns firing a long barrage. All of this was landing in an area 2, 500 yards deep and 6, 000 yards wide directly in front of the 9th Infantry Division positions. I felt that no one could be left alive in the area, and the Germans would all be knocked out. The 9th Infantry Division should be able to stroll through the German defenses.

We had quite a scare when the bombing stopped because some troops in the area started calling out, "Gas." It could have been that some of the bombs had hit a gas dump, but all the troops in the area thought the Germans were using poison gas to prevent a breakout. Everyone scrambled to find his gas mask. We all had gas masks but had never used them. They got in our way so they were not carried and were put away in the trucks. Because they were under other equipment, we had a hard time finding them. Some men had even thrown them away. It was fortunate that this was a false alarm, or we would have had a lot of casualties.

There was another problem. Some of the heavy bombers had dropped their load in the wrong place. They had bombed two battalions of the U.S. 9th Division ahead of us. This mistake had caused several hundred casualties and had disorganized the battalions. The attack had to be delayed. Another casualty was Gen. McNair, who was the commander of all the U.S. ground forces. He was here from the States to observe the bombing. He was killed when one of our bombs landed in his foxhole.

After the dead and wounded men were removed, the 9th Division went on to the attack.

Early the next day, the 18th Infantry Combat Team passed through the 47th Infantry Combat Team of the 9th Division and pushed through the German lines. By 0700 hours the following day, the 18th Infantry, after heavy fighting, had crossed the Périers–St. Lô road and was heading toward Marigny.

Our company left Haut Verney at 2330 hours, traveled by truck four miles and arrived at Les Champs de Losque at 0200 hours. The roads were good and the weather cloudy. The convoy was very slow because the roads had been clogged with the wreckage of burned-out German tanks and trucks. They had to be bulldozed off the roads by the engineers. The wreckage was piled up on the sides of the roads, along with the bodies of dead German soldiers. The Germans had suffered heavy casualties. We had few casualties.

We set up the aid station, and evacuation was underway although enemy shells were landing 300–500 yards ahead of the aid station.

July 27, 1944. Montreuil, France

Early on the 27th, the 18th Infantry units fought their way into Marigny and took this important crossroad. A combat team of the 3d Armored Division had bypassed Marigny on the right and had taken the important high ground north of Coutances. In doing so, soldiers found they were alone in the rear of a much larger German force to the north. To help them, patrols of the 16th Infantry found a small gap in the German lines and, at night, the entire 16th Infantry Combat Team slipped through a 300-yard gap down an old logging trail and fought its way to help the 3d Armored Division strengthen its position. They both went on to attack Coutances from the east.

On the evening of the 27th, elements of the 1st Division broke into the outskirts of Coutances, and the way for the breakout was cleared. This opened the way for the 4th Armored Division to come from the north, race down the coastal road, break out into the open and eventually go to Brittany.

Gen. Patton's 3d Army was now in operation. Many Germans were caught in a trap. The 1st Division's task was to move fast and keep the Germans contained. We left Les Champs de Losque at 1430 hours, and traveled 3½ miles to Montreuil by truck and arrived at 1530 hours. The roads and weather were good. Again, there was a tremendous number of burned-out German trucks and tanks all along the roads we traveled. The aid station was set up and operating as usual.

July 28–29, 1944. La Barberie, France.

We left Montreuil at 1400 hours and traveled by truck three miles to the vicinity of La Barberie, arriving at 1430 hours. The aid station was set up and operating. We were evacuating both American and German wounded.

The armored divisions of the newly activated U.S. 3d Army passed us in the night. As they roared by, I was awed by the huge number of tanks, trucks and equipment heading behind the German lines.

July 30, 1944. St. Denis-le-Gast (2½ miles northeast), France

We left La Barberie at 2230 hours and traveled by truck 18 miles, arriving at 0130 hours. The roads and weather were good. The aid station was set up and in operation.

Some of the German units were so demoralized that they were surrendering to any U.S. Army units near them. One of our litter bearers, Pvt. Lenihan, had three German paratroopers approach him and surrender. I am sure that it was the Red Cross armband that helped. They wanted to make sure they were not shot by mistake.

July 31, 1944. St. Denis-le-Gast (2½ miles northeast), France

The division crossed the Sienne river at Gavray. This advance had brought out the German air force at night. We had control of the air during the day but at night the Germans would sometimes bomb our areas, using clusters of anti-personnel bombs.

After dark, our company had packed up all our gear, and we were waiting in a field for word to move out. Although we had not seen any German planes for a long time, our trucks and ambulances were parked under trees to make sure we would not be detected by any enemy aircraft. It was a pleasant, warm evening, and we were not in artillery range so we did not dig foxholes. The moon was bright, and we sat around talking. About midnight, we were still waiting for orders to move when I heard the unmistakable throbbing sound of German JU-88 bombers. I hadn't heard that sound for a long time, and I started to shiver a little, and so did some of the other men. We remembered the many times the German JU-88s had bombed us in North Africa. The planes came closer until they were directly overhead. Then, I heard the screams of anti-personnel bombs coming down. Everyone dropped to the ground, into ditches or dived under trucks. The bombs were exploding all around, and I could hear men yelling as they got hit by bomb fragments.

I was lucky and did not get hit but men all around me had been wounded, and one of our trucks was on fire. The truck fire was quickly put out by Cpl. Marcavage, and we immediately attended to our wounded men. We then set up the aid station to care for the casualties from a nearby tank destroyer battalion. We also had to evacuate others in the 18th Infantry Combat Team who had been wounded in this bombing raid. The more seriously wounded men were evacuated, and the ones with minor wounds remained on duty. Nearby, Danger Forward, the advance division command post, was also hit. They had men both killed and wounded. The Germans were reacting to the serious defeat they had just suffered and were trying to prevent us from taking advantage of the breakout from the beachhead.

The men in our company who were wounded were T5 James G. Carney (evacuated), T5 Nick Dranzo (evacuated), Pfc. Edgar H. Drehle (evacuated), Pfc. Leonard S. Sterling (evacuated), Pfc. James S. Chrisafis (evacuated), Pfc. Arthur F. Doyle (evacuated), Pfc. Salvatore Ficara (evacuated), Pfc. Claude L. Rickerd (evacuated), S. Sgt. Jack Pingree (evacuated but returned the same day), S. Sgt. Walter A. Sherman (evacuated but returned the same day), S. Sgt. Ralph S. Weeks (evacuated but returned the same day), Lt. Alfonso M. Gaimari (remained on duty), Sgt. Kenneth K. Woods (remained on duty) and Pfc. Genero Riveria (remained on duty).

The next morning, I looked over our area in daylight and counted about 100 bomb holes in an area the size of an acre. Because of the large number of bombs in the small area, it seemed like no one could have survived. We were lucky. We had only 14 men wounded and one truck damaged out of our 90 men and 15 vehicles. It shows that quick reactions and lying on the ground can save a lot of lives.

August 1, 1944. Mesnil-Garnier
(¾ mile east), France

The bombing delayed our departure, and we left St. Denis-le-Gast at 1430 hours, traveled by truck eight miles and arrived at 1530 hours. The weather was good and so were the roads. We set up the aid station and evacuated the wounded as usual. The litter bearers were with the 18th Infantry Battalion.

The 18th Combat Team and Task Force X of the 3d Armored Division were given orders to attack and capture Brécey and the high ground around it. This was to be accomplished by noon. When this was done, the units were ordered to take the town of Mortain and be responsible for the left flank of the VII Army Corps.

Mortain was about 30 miles behind the German lines. We were now in back of the area we were at Caumont. The Germans were between us and the beachhead. The left side of the German line facing the beachhead had collapsed and the U.S. 3d Army was pouring through the gap. The VII Corps objective (we were now in the VII Corps) was to prevent the Germans from cutting off the U.S. 3d Army.

August 2, 1944. Brécey (2000 yards northwest), France

We left Mesnil-Garnier at 1030 hours, traveled by truck 14 miles and arrived at 1200 hours. The station was set up, and evacuation was proceeding normally. The 18th Infantry was not incurring many casualties but there were many German wounded and dead. We were evacuating mostly German wounded.

As the 1st Division moved farther east behind the Germans, who were facing the beachhead, other U.S. Army units would take up the positions we had left to form a ring around the Germans.

August 3–5, 1944. La Chevalaye (¼ mile west), France

We left Brécey at 1400 hours on August 3 and traveled ten miles by truck to the new area. The roads and weather were good. The aid station was set up and operating.

Mortain was captured by the 1st Division on the 3d of August. Because this was a strategic road junction, the division started to set up defensive positions in anticipation of a strong German counterattack. While this was going on, there was a lull in the fighting, so I took a few hours off. The jeep driver and I went a few miles to see Mont-Saint-Michel. I had always wanted to see it, and I found it to be as breathtaking as I had imagined. We did not have time to visit the monastery.

Before the defensive positions around Mortain were completed, orders came for the division and attached units of the 3d Armored Division and one combat team from the 9th Division to move fast and capture Mayenne. This was about 25 miles away in a southeasterly direction. The defensive positions around Mortain were turned over to the U.S. 30th Infantry Division as we prepared to move. During this period, German activity in our area was increasing. It was felt that they would attack Mortain in force. We were still moving farther behind the German lines.

The seriousness of our breakout had brought out the Luftwaffe (the German air force) in daylight. We had our first daylight attack in Europe. We were assembled in a field ready to move out when we heard rockets screaming overhead. They exploded in front of us. Seconds later, we saw a large flight of German planes, traveling extremely fast, zoom over low. Then we heard the tremendous roar of engines. We did not know what they were until we were told they were a new type of warplane powered by jet engines. They were the first jet planes we had ever seen. They were faster than all other planes. The sight of a new German plane much faster than anything we had was worrisome. I hoped that the Germans did not have many of them and that we had something to use against these planes. Our present fighter planes would probably have a difficult time against these jets.

Very little damage was done, and we did not receive any casualties. Maybe these planes were so new that they do not know how to get the most out of them.

August 6, 1944. Ambrières-le-Grand (2 miles west), France

We left La Chevalaye at 1800 hours, traveled by truck 32 miles and arrived at 2125 hours. The roads and the weather were good. The aid station was set up and in operation.

The aid station usually was ahead of the rest of the company because we traveled close to the attacking infantry battalions. We had no trouble with German patrols on the way. However, part of our company was on the road when they ran into a German patrol. One of our trucks and an ambulance were ambushed by the German patrol. They fired on the ambulance and truck with rifles and machine guns. In the melee, this group incurred some casualties. Our company had the following men wounded or missing as a result of this ambush: Lt. Joseph Gorniak (evacuated), T5 Lewis E. Randall (evacuated), Pvt. Carl W. Elsholz (evacuated), Pvt. Archie Watkins (evacuated), Pvt. Robert Winchester (evacuated), Sgt. Ralph Hogan (remained on duty), Pfc. Roy E. Gibson (remained on duty), Pvt. Adolf A. Allmoslecher (missing in action) and Pvt. John J. Fanale (missing in action).

August 7–12, 1944. Ambrières-le-Grand (2 miles west), France

The aid station was set up in a field just off the main road and was operating as usual. Shortly after we arrived, one of our men who had laid down to rest in the field, fell asleep. A truck pulled off the road and ran over both his legs. We thought that his legs had been broken, but the ground was soft, and the wheels had pushed his legs into the soft ground. He just had very severe bruises.

The 18th Infantry Combat Team was now way behind the German lines, and the German army was mounting a large armored attack at Mortain. It was about ten miles from Mortain to the Atlantic Ocean at the bay of Mont-Saint-Michel. If they could break through and reach the sea, they would cut off the entire U.S. 3d Army and the VII Army Corps from their supply lines.

The Germans attacked Mortain on the morning of August 7, with four Panzer divisions. The 30th U.S. Division, with help from the 4th Infantry Division, Allied aircraft and extra artillery, managed to contain the attack. The Canadians had also started an attack from the beachhead and that took pressure off the 30th Division.

In spite of this threat, the 1st Infantry Division and the 3d Armored Division kept attacking deeper into France and crossed the Mayenne river. The city of Mayenne was captured. The division then turned northeast toward La Ferté-Macé.

While the fierce battle was going on at Mortain, the situation east of Mortain, where we were, was quite unique. As the 1st Division expanded its position with the aid of the attached combat team from the 9th Division, it was engaged in fighting on three sides. The attached combat team from 9th Division was attacking north. The main body of the division was moving south, and the left flank of the division was under pressure from the Germans from the east.

August 13, 1944. La Sorriers, France

We left Ambrières at 0900 hours and traveled by truck 12 miles to the new location. We arrived at 2330 hours. The roads on this trip were clogged with burned-out German tanks and vehicles. We also saw many dead horses still attached to their wagons and, of course, many dead German soldiers. I was amazed at the number of horses used by the German army. I had thought that it was entirely mechanized. Most of this destruction was a result of our fighter bombers, which caught the German convoys in the open on the roads and bombed and strafed without letup.

The aid station was set up and in operation.

August 14, 1944. La Chapelle-Moche, France

We left La Sorriers at 1800 hours and traveled 3½ miles, arriving at 1830 hours. The roads were excellent. We were not finding many of the enemy in this swing around the rear of the German lines and thus there were not many casualties. Because there was little opposition from the German army, I wondered why the division was not attacking to close the ring on the German 7th army. We were told that the British army was going to close the noose of the trap. We were not to attack because we might fire on the British and they might fire on us.

On August 14, I received copies of two 1st Division general orders. No. 62, dated 12 August 1944, stated the award of the Bronze Star medal to Allen N. Towne:

> For heroic achievement in connection with military operations against the enemy in the vicinity of Vierville-sur-Mer, Normandy, France, June 6, 1944. Voluntarily exposing himself to heavy artillery and small-arms fire, Sergeant Towne fearlessly moved about open terrain, administering first-aid and evacuating wounded men. His heroic devotion to duty saved many lives.

No. 64, dated 14 August 1944, stated the award of the Oak Leaf Cluster to the Bronze Star medal to Allen N. Towne:

> For heroic achievement in the vicinity of Cormolain, Normandy, France, June 25, 1944. Voluntarily subjecting himself to severe bombardment, Sergeant Towne crossed wide areas of open terrain, treating a number of seriously wounded men. Sergeant Towne's heroic devotion to duty reflects great credit on the Medical Department.

August 15–23, 1944. St. Michel-les-Andaines (2 miles north), France

We left the last area at 2015 hours and traveled seven miles by truck, arriving at 2300 hours. The roads and weather were good. The aid station was set up and operating.

The combat team had not been in contact with the enemy since August 18th. We had been squeezed out of the perimeter of the pocket that held the trapped German 7th Army. The British did not close the noose until many of the Germans had escaped.

The division was now ordered to change direction and proceed north, going through Couterne, Bagnoles and La Ferté-Macé. This would require consolidating our positions and some resupplying before making that long move. We were able to relax, clean up and replenish medical supplies. We also attended a USO show and a new movie (at least new to us). For the first and only time, we had a visit from a Red Cross cubmobile. They gave us each a free doughnut. Our own cooks provided the coffee.

We had our aid station in a big old mansion (or chateau). It was set up in the large entrance hall, where we had a lot of room for litters. The rest of the company were in other rooms. We thought it was nice to have plush accommodations.

When we were packing up to leave, a pompous rear-echelon colonel and his staff wanted us to get out so they could move in. The colonel was very impressed by his own importance and imperiously told us we should move out fast. He also had a little pet poodle he kept near him. He was very concerned about the dog's comfort and well-being. He gave us so much trouble that we got a little rankled. I decided to take him down a peg, so I slipped a Nembutol (a sleeping capsule) in the poodle's mouth. In about a half hour, the poodle was acting drunk and staggering around. The colonel thought the dog was really sick. He was so upset he asked us if we could find out what was wrong. I told the colonel that we did not know much about dogs but we would look at him. One of our men, who had worked with a veterinarian before he was drafted, took the dog and stuck a thermometer in the dog's mouth and said the dog had a fever. Finally, when the dog went to sleep, we told the colonel that the dog was in a coma, and we left.

Fourteen

Race through France and Belgium

August 24, 1944. Courville, France

The division was now ordered to move quickly northeast and cross the Seine river upstream from Paris (near Melun and Corbeil). We left St. Michel-les-Andaines at 1700 hours, traveled by truck 110 miles and arrived in Courville, in the vicinity of Chartres, at 2400 hours. The roads and weather were good. There was no action on the way, and so we did not set up the aid station. We had ambulances with the 18th Infantry Battalion and they would send any sick directly back to the clearing company.

August 25–26, 1944. Cerney
(1000 yards west), France

We left Courville at 0830 and traveled 70 miles by truck and arrived at 1400 hours. There was no hostile action in the vicinity but we set up the aid station to take care of the sick. We evacuated to the division clearing company.

These were heady times for us. We felt that it was possible that the war in Europe would soon be over because it looked like the Germans were retreating in disorder. We might be able to stop the remnants of the German army in France before they could get organized. The weather was warm, the sky clear and the countryside showed little effect of the war. We felt like we were on a motor trip through a very friendly country. When we would pass through cities and towns, people would wave and cheer.

At night, we did not expect any casualties, and we did not dig foxholes. We would just take off our shoes and wrap up in a blanket and lay down on the ground and sleep.

August 27, 1944. Gretz, France

We left Cerney at 1000 hours and traveled to an area near Corbeil, which is on the Seine river downstream from Melun. Our convoy went into a nice residential area, which was quite heavily populated. We parked our vehicles along the wide street in front of large brick houses. We waited there for many hours because the division had to queue up to cross the Seine river. They were using a pontoon bridge the engineers had put up over the Seine river near Corbeil. All the old bridges had been blown up by our bombers. We were about 20 miles south/southeast of Paris.

The French people came out of their houses to talk to us, and they were very friendly. Many of the people could speak English. They offered us bread (very good, hard French bread) and wine. We reciprocated with candy and cigarettes. They were happy to see that the war was over for them and they no longer were under German rule.

I was surprised that there were so many young men there but it made sense because France had been out of the war for several years. It was more profitable for the Germans to have the French people work in industry and help supply their war effort.

After a long wait, we crossed the Seine at 1530 hours via the one-lane pontoon bridge. The crossing was time-consuming because the heavy trucks and tanks had to move slowly over the long bridge. It was constructed using a series of boats placed side-by-side across the river. Then, the engineers laid a wood plank road over a frame built on the boats. The parts had all been prepared a long time ago, and it was similar to assembling an erector set.

We arrived in Gretz-Armainvilliers at 1800 hours. It had taken us ten hours to go the 35 miles from Cerney to Gretz. We were now about 20 miles east of Paris.

August 28, 1944. Boutigny (1000 yards southwest), France

We left Gretz at 1425 hours and traveled by truck 23 miles and arrived at 1600 hours. The roads were good, and the convoy traveled fast. We were now going north-northwest and leaving the Paris area, heading toward Laon. There was no real organized resistance from the German army, although there were now quite a few German soldiers around. Many of them were surrendering to any American soldier they could find. Three Germans surrendered to one of our officers in Gretz.

Waiting to cross the Seine river on a pontoon bridge near Melun, France. *Left to right:* Sgt. McFarland, French civilian, Pvt. Miller.

August 29, 1944. Brumetz (about 45 miles northeast of Paris), France

We left Boutigney at 0930 hours and traveled 27 miles and arrived at 1300 hours. The roads and weather were good, and the convoy was reasonably fast. The 3d Armored Division was ahead of us, and the 18th Infantry Regimental Combat Team was on the left flank of the 1st Division going through France. The 9th Infantry Division was on the right flank of the three-division column.

The way we were fighting the Germans made me think of how the German army broke through the Allied lines early in the war, when they went through Belgium, Holland and France. The Germans called it blitzkrieg, and now we had the U.S. Army blitzkrieg. It was almost in the same location as the German army victory in 1940.

All units were in continual movement, and we had complete command of the air. The 3d Armored Division had units way out in front of us and was causing confusion and panic in the advance units of the estimated 120,000 enemy troops still remaining south of the Belgian border. These enemy troops were trying to get to the German border before they were cut off.

We had good communication because we had command of the air and knew where the Germans were. The German units had no idea where we were.

We had a flight of 12 P-47 fighter bombers overhead most of the daylight hours. If any German forces were sighted, the field artillery would pull off the road and start firing without digging in their guns. If help was needed by the fighter bombers, the air force had air controllers with the infantry units, and they would call for immediate air strikes. We would see the planes come in low to bomb and strafe the Germans who were just ahead of us.

Now, we would only set up a skeleton aid station unless a heavy skirmish would take place. We were evacuating to our clearing company although it sometimes was a long way off.

August 30, 1944. Bucy-de-Long, France

We left Brumetz at 0830 and traveled 31 miles, arriving at 2000 hours. We had now crossed the Marne river and were near Soissons, where the 1st Division fought a big battle in World War I. In four days, the division had suffered 8,500 casualties in this battle.

August 31, 1944. Laon (4 miles south), France

We left Bucy-de-Long at 1030 hours and traveled 22 miles to a new area, arriving at 1300 hours. The roads and the weather were good. The aid station was set up and operating. Only scattered resistance was made by the Germans. There still did not seem to be any organized resistance. What resistance occurred was quickly dealt with. This resulted in many prisoners and a few wounded German soldiers. We had almost no U.S. casualties. There was a great deal of wrecked German equipment on the roads as a result of our air strikes.

Many of the enemy units had left behind vast amounts of materiel, gasoline and food. Some of our infantry companies were living off the best of the German rations. The disorganization of the Germans was so bad that one group of 390 German prisoners were from 24 different German army units.

September 1, 1944. Toulis, France

We left Laon and traveled 15 miles, arriving at 1445 hours. The aid station was set up and in operation.

September 2, 1944. Leschelle, France

We left Toulis at 1415 hours and traveled 27 miles, arriving at 1700 hours. The road and weather were good. We were now seeing more enemy activity, and the artillery was pulling off to the side of the road more often to fire. There was also more activity by the P-47s, which were flying above the column. They would go ahead and bomb and strafe. We were also getting more German wounded into the aid station. Our casualties were still light.

The 3d Armored Division was quite far ahead of the 1st Division. There were no friendly troops within 25 miles. The division was spread out over a large area and was starting to have a problem keeping the vehicles supplied with gasoline. It was a long distance to the gas depots. The quartermaster troops were laying a gasoline pipeline from the beachhead toward Paris. When this was completed, it should help to alleviate the gasoline shortage. Gen. Bradley had also taken trucks from a newly arrived armored division and was using them to supply the fast-moving troops. At the same time, the Army supply was setting up a huge trucking unit, called the "Red Ball Express," which operated a large fleet of trucks day and night.

September 3–5, 1944. Malgarni, France

We left the last area at 1030 hours and traveled 30 miles to Malgarni, arriving at 1600 hours. The roads and weather were good but the column had

Sgt. McFarland at a signpost in France near Mons, Belgium.

to make frequent stops as we were running into more German troops. We were now very near to the Belgian border and close to the Belgian city of Mons and about 70 miles from the Atlantic coast. The aid station was set up, and we were busy but with more German wounded than our own. The division was now traveling in parallel columns of combat teams, heading for the German border.

The 3d Armored Division had pushed a long finger north of the 1st Division and into Belgium, east of Mons. They were cutting across the intended escape route of five German divisions. Three of the divisions were moving into the 1st Division's line of march, and the other two were retreating on the left. Our intelligence had determined that these German divisions had been directed to make an orderly withdrawal and to occupy the Siegfried line near Aachen before the Americans could get there. They were elements of the 15th German Army, which had been stationed at Pas de Calais. They were trying to get back to Germany before they were cut off.

With the German 15th Army were elements of what was left of the German 7th Army, which was almost destroyed in Normandy. In this group, there were parts of 20 German divisions trying to get back to Germany. The retreat route of the 15th German Army led through the city of Mons, just across the French border in Belgium. The 15th German Army units were marching back to Germany in an administrative march rather than in formations prepared for combat. The army had left Pas de Calais around the end of August, a few days after the fall of Paris.

As the 1st Division moved north toward Mons, it ran directly into the flank of this German force. The battle that followed resulted in one of the worst defeats the German Army suffered in France. All elements of the division, including the division artillery, division headquarters and the engineers, were engaged in close combat. This action kept the aid station very busy but most of the casualties were Germans.

About 6,000 Germans were killed or wounded and more than 17,000 prisoners were taken in four days by the 1st Division alone. The 3d Armored Division took additional thousands of prisoners. In this battle, four German divisions were largely destroyed and two others badly hurt. There were very few casualties in our combat team and in the division as a whole. This happened because we had the air superiority and knew where the Germans were. They were blind and walked into our traps.

There was one highway where the spectacle sickened all of us, and we had seen a lot of horrible sights over the past two years. A very long double column of Germans had been moving east towards Germany. It had filled the entire wide highway when it was spotted by an American fighter bomber formation. The planes came down and strafed the long German army column from end to end. At the same time, our artillery saw what the planes were doing and pulled off the road and zeroed in on the helpless Germans. After

German soldiers dead in field near Mons, Belgium.

that, all that needed to be done was to take prisoners and take care of the wounded German soldiers who survived. The highway was impassable due to the wreckage. After the fires died down, the road was bulldozed clear by the engineers.

Later, the Belgian civilians collected the dead Germans in large piles so they could be buried in mass graves. We were very glad we did not have to do this like we used to in North Africa.

September 6, 1944. Loveral (near Charleroi), Belgium

We left Malgarni at 1600 hours and traveled 35 miles to the new area in Belgium. We arrived at 1900 hours. The weather and roads were good, but the traveling was slow because the roads were filled with burned-out vehicles, burned-out tanks, dead horses and dead German soldiers. Perhaps the worst sight (except for the dead soldiers) were the dead horses all stiff, with their feet sticking out straight. They were still attached to the guns and wagons.

German soldiers dead near Mons, Belgium.

When we went through the large city of Charleroi, the people all came out in the streets to cheer us on. We stopped for a few hours in Charleroi, and the people were so overjoyed they invited us into their homes to sit down and talk and have some bread and wine.

Dead German soldiers being collected by Belgian civilians.

September 7, 1944. Namur, Belgium

We left Loveral at 1100 hours and traveled 22 miles arriving, at 1430 hours. The roads and weather were good. We did not set up the aid station here or Loveral because all the Germans in the vicinity had either surrendered or had taken off for the German border.

We now had a severe problem because we were so far away from our supply lines that our vehicles were running out of gasoline. The 3d Armored Division probably could have pushed right into Germany in force but it did not have enough gas to sustain such a move. We hoped that we could get gas and other supplies in time to get far into Germany before the German army had time to regroup and set up defenses.

September 8–9, 1944. St. Georges, Belgium

We left Namur and traveled 28 miles, arriving at 1400 hours. Because of lack of gasoline, we were not pushing ahead.

Fifteen

Aachen

We left St. Georges at 1030 hours and traveled 28 miles. The roads and weather were good. The aid station was set up and was in operation as usual.

On September 5, 1944, Gen. Eisenhower had decided that the U.S. forces should advance rapidly to the Rhine river by going through the Aachen gap in the north and the Metz gap in the south. The 1st Division was in the north, so the attack was on to capture Aachen. This was the famous old capital of Charlemagne. About 160,000 people lived in Aachen in 1939. Now, it was estimated there were about 20–25,000 civilians living in the city. It had been hit with over 50 large-scale air raids, and many buildings had been destroyed and most of the civilians had left the city. Aachen was one of those border cities that had belonged to various countries over the centuries. It had another name, Aix-La-Chapelle, that was used when it belonged to France and later when it belonged to Belgium.

We were in the part of Belgium that was very close to both the German and Dutch borders. Our ambulances had to go to all the units of the 18th Infantry Combat Team. This meant they were traveling in all three countries. I went with an ambulance into Holland, and we visited a shoe manufacturer, where I bought a pair of new shoes. The shoes were just the type you would need in the muddy fields around here. They were easy to slip off when going into a house. They were "sabots," or wooden shoes. The factory where they were made was interesting. They would start with a large block of wood, and with a special machine, cut out the inside of the shoe. Then, with another machine, finish the outside. The shoes I bought did not have any straps to hold them on my feet. I had a difficult time keeping them on because they were loose-fitting so I sent them home as a souvenir.

The 1st Division was given the task of capturing Aachen with help from the 30th Infantry Division on the left and the 3d Armored Division on the right. On September 11, the 18th Infantry Combat Team was ordered to attack the Siegfried line in the vicinity of Aachen. The Siegfried line was the fortified

137

border of Germany. It consisted of tank barriers called dragon's teeth. They were rows of reinforced concrete posts of uneven shapes and heights, with some as high as three feet. There were five parallel rows extending as far as you could see. In front of the dragon's teeth was a parallel ditch about 10–15 feet deep that was camouflaged. This was also a tank barrier. Behind these barriers there were many reinforced concrete pillboxes, where artillery and machine guns would be mounted. The Germans had permanent troops manning the Siegfried line as well as mobile troops available to counterattack in places that needed help.

September 12–13, 1944. Aubel, Belgium

We left Herve at 1430 hours and went six miles, arriving at 1515 hours. The roads and weather were good. The aid station was set up, and evacuation was proceeding normally.

On the 12th, the attack by the 18th Infantry was met with stubborn resistance, although the 16th Infantry on our right had broken through the Siegfried line and captured many pillboxes. That night, it was dark before I had time to pick out a spot to unroll my blanket and go to sleep. I went 10-15 feet away from the aid station and laid down. In the morning, when it became light, I found that I was sleeping right next to an unexploded eight-inch artillery shell. I moved to a different spot the following night. We also moved the aid station away from the shell.

The attack continued on the 13th and, finally, the 18th Infantry Combat Team took the high ground west of the Aachen-Liege road. It had completely broken through the Siegfried line in this area. However, in the Aachen area, the Siegfried line had two lines of fortifications that were somewhat parallel but miles apart. This meant that, sometime, the other section had to be taken.

September 14–16, 1944. Montzen, Belgium

The company left Aubel at 1030 hours and traveled seven miles, arriving at 1115 hours. The roads and weather were good. The aid station was set up, and evacuation was proceeding normally.

On the 14th, the 26th Infantry Combat Team also breached the Siegfried line and so had the 3d Armored Division on the right of the 1st Division. The Germans had taken advantage of the delays caused by the gasoline shortages to bring in reinforcements. In addition to the three fortress battalions they had defending Aachen, they had brought up two new units (the 523d Infantry and the GAF Battalion). This made it more difficult for us to advance, and there was a high probability of counterattacks. This meant higher casualties.

September 17–October 7, 1944. Hergenrath, Belgium

We left Montzen and traveled four miles, arriving at 1415 hours. The roads and weather were good. The ambulances and litter bearers were with the 18th Infantry because the division had been ordered to assist the 3d Armored Division in capturing Stolberg and Munsterbusch. This meant another attack and more casualties. The plan was to encircle Aachen and then ask the German military commander to surrender the city. If the Germans refused, the 1st Division was to take Aachen by force.

The aid station was set up in a house near the outskirts of Herganrath, a little Belgian town on the German border. The house we were in had been abandoned. We were told that the owners were German sympathizers and had left when the forward units of the 3d Armored Division came into the area.

The weather was still good but it was starting to get cool, especially at night. We felt it would be hard to keep a tent warm, so we had looked for a suitable house. In all the years we had been operating our aid station, we had rarely been in a house. We normally would set up our aid station outside in good weather or in a tent in bad weather. The reason for this was we were always on the move and, except for a few days in the mountains of Tunisia, we never experienced real cold weather.

During a battle, we knew many of the wounded men would be in or near shock, and we had to keep them warm. We also had to keep the blood plasma warm. We did not require much room for equipment but we did need room for the wounded men on litters. Our standard setup was two chests (the size of a trunk) standing on end about seven feet apart. On each chest, we would fasten a bracket to hold one end of a litter. When a wounded man on a litter was placed on the chests, he would be at the proper height to work on. It was, in effect, an operating table. We had two such setups. The chests contained all the necessary instruments and supplies. Of course, we also carried large quantities of blankets and litters.

The town of Herganrath did not have a doctor, so we were called on to provide medical aid to the civilians, especially the very young and very old. The makeup of the population was much different from what it was in France. In France, you would see many civilian men. Here, even though it was Belgium, we did not see any men between the ages of 20 and 60. Perhaps, because it was on the German border, most of the men were of German extraction and were in the German army.

Once, we were asked to help an old woman who had a bad angina attack.

Her main problem was that she had run out of nitroglycerine tablets and had no way to get more. We gave her a supply and visited her several times to see if she improved. She did. We also were called to help women with young children. We would treat them as required and sometimes gave shots of penicillin. The procedure in these cases would be that a doctor and I would go to their house the first time. If a further visit was required, I would go alone.

Being near a friendly town for about 20 days had one fringe benefit. Our cooks could trade flour for Belgian bread. The Belgians make excellent hard rolls and bread.

On September 17, the operation called Market Garden was initiated. This was a British attack toward Germany through Holland with the objective of crossing the Rhine river to the German border. They expected there would only be a small defense line (not like the heavily fortified Siegfried line in front of us). This operation diverted supplies from our front, and we were now severely rationed in gasoline and ammunition. Thus, the effectiveness of the 1st Division and the 3d Armored Division was curtailed. This allowed the Germans to build up their force to about triple the size of a month ago.

On September 17, the Germans counterattacked the division with part of the 12th German division, which had been withdrawn from the Russian front. It had been reorganized and re-equipped and sent to Dueren by train to protect and defend Aachen. The counterattack was repulsed, and the Germans suffered very large losses. One wounded German who was captured made this statement about the battle: "We have been three years on the Russian front and we have been beaten before. However, this is the first time we have ever been stopped by small-arms fire."*

In the middle of September, winter clothes were issued, and because the line was somewhat stable, we were able to take showers and attend a movie.

On September 27, two men from our company previously reported missing in action (Allmoslecher and Fanale) were reported to have died of wounds on August 10, 1944.

October 8–11, 1944. Ober Forstbach, Germany

We left Herganrath at 0800 hours and traveled seven miles to the new area, arriving at 0845 hours. The roads and weather were good. The aid station was set up for the first time in Germany. Evacuation was proceeding normally.

Goebbels had promised that Aachen would be Germany's "Stalingrad," and Hitler said Aachen would be defended to the end. All civilians were ordered out of the city.

---

*Quoted in H.B. Knickerbocker et al., Danger Forward: The Story of the First Division in World War II (Washington, D.C.: Society of the First Division, 1947), page 281.

The quick and easy attack on Aachen had not succeeded so, after regrouping, the 18th Infantry Regimental Combat Team was given the task of capturing the town of Verlautenheide. Then they were to capture hill 239. We called it "Crucifix Hill" because of the large wooden cross on the top. Although, later, it had a more somber meaning. After Crucifix Hill was taken they were to go on and take hill 231, called Ravelsberg. This was only a short distance, two or three miles, but it was loaded with pillboxes. The Germans had the hills for observation and could lay their artillery with precision on the attacking 18th Infantry. This advance would put the 18th Infantry almost in back of the city of Aachen. This would allow the 30th Division on the left of Aachen to make a junction with the 18th, and the city would be surrounded.

October 12–November 9, 1944. Brand, Germany

Because we expected the battle for Aachen would result in many casualties, we moved our aid station closer to the action. The litter bearers were with the infantry battalions, and our company headquarters and service units remained behind. We left Ober Forstbach at 1300 hours and traveled 3½ miles to Brand. Brand was a residential section of Aachen.

The houses in Germany seemed to be built better than the ones we had seen in Belgium and even France. The area we were in now was very prosperous-looking. The aid station was set up in a modern house. It was built like a split-level house and had a garage under part of the house at road level. This was ideal for an aid station because the ambulances could come right up to the aid station. It would be easy to load the litters into the ambulances. The house was easy to keep warm because it was well-built and insulated. The weather was cold and rainy so it was nice to be able to keep warm. There was no electricity in any of the houses because the power lines had been blown out a long time ago, and no one would dare to try to repair them.

The fighting was close to us, and most civilians had left. They must have left in a hurry because the house we were in was completely furnished. There were many framed photographs of the family hung on the walls. However, there still were some civilians in the area. We had not been there very long when an older man came to the aid station and asked for help. A woman in his family was expecting a baby and was in labor. Because there were no German medical people around, he asked if we would help. It was late in the afternoon and was quite dark so we were not sure we should go. The German said he lived nearby. He also said the woman was old to have a baby, and he was concerned about possible problems.

One of the doctors (who had been an obstetrician in civilian practice) and I went with the man to a house several blocks away. We went into the cellar of an older house. The cellar was completely underground and had steel beams supporting the upper floor, which was a thick slab of poured concrete. It was like a real large bomb shelter and ideal for shell-fire defense. I later found that many houses in this area were built this way. It could be that they have had so many wars here that they always build shelters in the basements.

In the cellar we found the woman who was in labor. The doctor examined her and said she should deliver within two or three hours. We had some coffee with us and spent the greater part of the night drinking coffee and waiting for the baby to arrive. There were no complications, and the birth was normal and uneventful. The only service we performed was to tie off the cord in two places and cut it. The doctor examined the baby, and it was normal. I had mixed up a silver nitrate solution, and the doctor put some drops into the baby's eyes. We then waited for the placenta to come out. The doctor examined it closely. It was intact and everything was normal, so we went back to the aid station.

The 18th Infantry captured Verlautenheide in a night attack and then went on to capture Crucifix Hill. Crucifix Hill was a high point overlooking the city of Aachen. The infantry company that took Crucifix Hill was led by Capt. Bobby Brown, who was a familiar face in the aid station. In this battle, he was wounded for the third or fourth time. He was wounded many more times and, after the seventh time, I don't believe he came back. This time, he had been riding on the radiator of a jeep, looking for mines. However, one had been hidden so well he did not see it, and it exploded under the jeep. He was badly burned and had other wounds. We did what we could to make him comfortable and sent him back to a field hospital. Capt. Brown was later awarded the Congressional Medal of Honor.

The next night, Ravelsberg was taken by the 18th Infantry. The 1st Battalion of the 18th Infantry was awarded a presidential unit citation for outstanding performance of duty in and around the city of Aachen and for the fighting on Crucifix Hill.

Thus, Aachen was almost surrounded and, on October 10, an ultimatum was given to the German commander in Aachen by the 1st Division commanding officer, Gen. Huebner. Aachen was to surrender within 24 hours or an immediate aerial and artillery bombardment would start, and Aachen would be destroyed. It was estimated there were about 5,000 German soldiers still in Aachen. We heard that Field Marshal von Rundstedt told the Aachen commander to hold Aachen to the last man. On the 11th, no word had been received from the Germans, so the bombardment started.

Our fighter bombers would come over in flights of 12 planes, and we could see them dropping their bombs on the buildings. They would start at one end of a street and bomb one building at a time until they had destroyed all of the street. Then, they would start on the next street. The artillery also started firing and continued all day.

Late in the day on the 11th, the Germans made a tank and infantry attack

Destruction from the battle to capture Aachen.

on the 18th Infantry positions on Crucifix Hill. It was repulsed. However, the 18th suffered many casualties, and we were kept busy. Some of our own men, who were carrying the wounded men back, were also hit, including Sgt. Marcus R. Nixon (shell fragment, in left leg), Pvt. Herald E. Vose (shell fragment wound, left cheek, remained on duty), Pvt. Clifford G. Carton (gunshot wound, left leg).

On October 12, the remainder of the company joined us at Brand. The 26th Infantry Regiment started an attack to clean out Aachen street by street on the 12th of October. They were using 155-mm rifles (heavy artillery) on tractor mounts to blow up pillboxes and other strong points in their way. While the 26th Infantry was cleaning out the 5,000 Germans still in Aachen, the 16th and 18th Infantry Regiments consolidated their positions.

The Germans in Aachen fought ferociously, and there was no retreat. It was house-to-house fighting. The infantry would use 2½ pounds of dynamite to blast their way through walls of buildings and would go through entire sections of the city without going outside. In one incident, where there was a steep hill going down to the center of the city, the engineers loaded a streetcar with explosives. It was on the track at the top of the hill. They rolled it down the hill, where it blew up.

We had a battery of 155-mm Long Toms in the back of the house where the aid station was set up. When they started shooting, it would almost blow out our eardrums. The artillery battery also attracted some of the few German planes in the vicinity. One night, we had a German fighter bomber drop a number of bombs within 25 feet of the house. They were large bombs, and they hit so close that some of the windows in our house had the glass sucked out. Other windows had the glass blown into the house. Needless to say, all of us were in the corners of the cellar until the bombers had finished. We did not have any casualties, and neither did the artillery men. We were just scared.

The 30th Division had a lot of trouble making the final link to complete the encirclement of Aachen. It was not until October 16 that the gap was closed. The Germans mounted some ferocious counterattacks to try to keep the gap open, and a lot of this pressure was on Crucifix Hill and Ravelsberg. The 18th Infantry suffered a lot of casualties, and had a number of the litter bearers in our company were wounded in some of these actions, especially in and around Crucifix Hill. On October 18, Pvt. Ezra K. Waldrop was wounded (shell fragment, left hand). On October 20, Pvt. John Mancino had a concussion from a shell landing nearby. On October 21, T5 Frank Fawcett received phosphorus burns on his face and hands from an enemy shell.

During this period, we were having quite a few men come in with anxiety state (a complete breakdown). Even some of our own men were breaking down. This happened to some of the men who had been wounded before and had returned. These men with anxiety state were never considered as battle casualties but rather as sick men. I often wondered if this was fair because somehow anxiety state leaves a stigma. Some of these men had been in tough combat for years and finally the continual stress broke them.

One of the platoon leaders, T. Sgt. Max Thompson of K Company of the 18th Infantry, was awarded the Congressional Medal of Honor for his exploits in the battle for Aachen. The award states:

> On the morning of October 18, the Germans made a heavy counterattack to drive the 3d Battalion of the 18th off a hill named "Ravels. B." They had a heavy artillery barrage for an hour and their infantry came in one of the biggest attacks the Third Battalion had ever seen. There were many tanks and halftracks. The weather was wet, muddy and cold. It was so bad that some of the weapons would not work. Sgt. Thompson led a squad against a machine gun and he knocked out the crew. All day long he was active. He personally knocked out two tanks with rifle grenades and a bazooka. He was still going that night even though the German attack had failed. He led a night patrol to capture the last German pillbox and succeeded.*

On October 21, 1944, Aachen surrendered. It was the first sizable German city to fall in World War II and it was in the middle of one of the most heavily fortified positions in the west wall. It was also a fortress city under personal orders from Hitler to hold at any cost.

---

*Source: The Decoy Doughboy (newspaper printed in Czechoslovakia by 18th Infantry Combat Team, May 23, 1945).

Sixteen

Bloody Hürtgen

November 10–15, 1944. Brand, Germany

On November 10, the division moved out of contact with the German army for the first time since the regrouping before the breakout around St. Lô in July. During this time, a few of us had an opportunity to go to a stage show held in a nearby school auditorium. We saw Marlene Dietrich, who sang many of the popular songs and even "Lily Marlene." This was the song of Rommel's Afrika Korps, and it became a favorite of the 1st Division in North Africa and Sicily. I went to the show with Cpl. Randall, and we were able to get seats in the first row. When Marlene Dietrich asked for a soldier to volunteer to sing with her, Cpl. Randall immediately jumped up and accepted. He was more than a match for her. He made advances to her, but it was all in good fun. We thought she showed a lot of courage performing this close to the fighting. Because she was a German, I imagined that if she was captured by the Nazis, she would be treated badly.

The break from action lasted for about six hours while the units of the division moved a few miles from around Aachen to the Vicht and Mousbach area for the forthcoming attack toward the Roer river. The 1st Division was to make the major effort of the U.S. VII Army Corps and attack in the direction of the town of Langerwehe and to cross the Rur (in Dutch, Roer) river north of Düren. The first objective of the attack was to take the town of Gressenich and the Hamrich-Nothberg ridge. A large part of this area was in the Hürtgen forest.

We knew that the fighting in the Hürtgen forest would be difficult because we had heard about the terrible losses other divisions had experienced in the Hürtgen forest. Even the 9th Division, which had been with us in North Africa and Normandy, had suffered heavy casualties.

Everyone was feeling low. We had all had quite a letdown from the days when we were racing through France and Belgium and thought the war would soon end. Now, the Germans were fighting as hard as they were before the breakout in Normandy. It seemed like the war would go on forever. We had been in action for two years, and most of us, especially the infantrymen, had lost hope that we would ever get back to the States in one piece. All of us were despondent. Some of this feeling was due to the time of year. The weather was rainy and cold and the woods thick and dark. Many of the roads were narrow and muddy, and the days were short. To make things even worse, the men did not have the proper winter clothes. There was a great need for warm, waterproof boots. The area of our attack was particularly good for the Germans to defend, and we knew they would take every advantage of the terrain.

Directly in front, they held a commanding hill that could be used to direct artillery fire. In the east, the thick woods of the Hürtgen forest were ideal for defense. The Germans had a lot of artillery. They had about 200 artillery pieces that could fire on any part of the division. This was about equal to the number we had available to us. The Germans were well dug in behind minefields and barbed-wire entanglements.

The offensive was planned to take the U.S. 1st Army to the Rhine river. It began at 1245 hours on November 16 with a saturation bombing of the German lines. The bombing started with a run of 1,200 heavy bombers from the U.S. 8th Air Force. This was followed by an equal number of heavy bombers from the British air force. The immense air bombardment churned up a lot of ground and may have killed some German soldiers, but it did not have the effect intended. It did not blow a hole through the German lines. The attack would have to go ahead the hard way by the infantry taking the high ground.

November 16–22, 1944. Zweifall, Germany

We left Brand at 1330 hours on the 16th and traveled seven miles to Zweifall, arriving at 1400 hours. On the way, we went through the part of Aachen where there had been a great deal of bombing and street fighting by the 1st Division. There was utter devastation in Aachen. In some places, it was hard to see where the streets had been. Bulldozers had to clear a way so the trucks could get through.

This time, the aid station was set up in a house on the east side of the small town of Zweifall. We were a few miles from the center of town and on a road that led in the direction of Wenau. We were not very far from Düren, an important road junction and railhead due west of Cologne (in German: Köln). The German army was using Düren as a supply base.

The house we were using had been abandoned. All the other houses in the area were empty, and it did not take long to find out why. Another unit, a combat group, had set up in a house about a quarter of a mile away. Several days after we moved in, we saw the house being shelled and, finally, it caught fire. However, none of the shells hit near us. Perhaps, whoever was shelling could see the ambulances and left us alone.

Destruction from the battle to take Aachen.

The weather was getting colder, and the rainy season had started. Because the combat team was not fully prepared for cold weather, we started to get men in the aid station with trenchfoot. Trenchfoot is caused by persistent dampness or immersion of the feet in water. It can result in permanent damage to the peripheral vessels of the lower limbs. It could incapacitate some soldiers for the rest of their lives. I guess this lack of proper shoes was due to the crisis in supply, caused by our fast advance through France, Belgium and up to the German border.

The losses in manpower among the infantry were high, and replacements were hard to get. Maybe people back in the States thought the European war was over and all the men and supplies were going to the Pacific area.

We also heard horrible stories about our own wounded who, after recovering from their wounds, would be sent to replacement depots to await transportation back to their units. Some of the men coming back would tell of the harsh treatment in these depots. They were treated like prisoners and kept inside barbed-wire enclosures. They were even beaten if they gave the depot people a hard time. Some were not even given blankets in this cold weather. Because of this, many of the men went AWOL and hitched rides back to their units even though they knew that they would be right back in action. This problem was finally cleared up and some of the people running the replacement depots were court-martialed.

At night, we could hear the British night bombers going over to bomb Cologne and Düren. We would see the red glow from the fires that burned all night. Yet, with all of the bombing, the Germans had plenty of ammunition, and German reinforcements were still arriving.

On November 20, the 18th Infantry Combat Team started the attack in the Hürtgen forest. A disastrous incident occurred before the attack started. One of the trucks carrying an infantry company to the attack area had just unloaded the men when a German shell hit a tree branch over their heads. The hot steel shell fragments killed 18 men instantly. Others were wounded, and we got them in the aid station a short time later. This was an omen of what was to come.

Later in the day, after a fierce battle, the 18th Infantry, with the help of an attached unit of 155-mm self-propelled artillery, captured the town of Wenau.

November 23–30, 1944. Vicht, Germany

The aid station left the remainder of the company on the 22d and set up in Vicht. This was 2½ miles from Zweifall.

On the 24th, the 18th Infantry took the high ground near Langerwehe. The Germans reacted by subjecting the position to intense mortar and artillery fire and then mounting a powerful counterattack. The Germans retook part of the high ground. The Germans and the 18th Infantry were both on the hill. The fighting went back and forth for four days until, finally, the Germans were driven off the hill. This battle of the Hürtgen forest was a battle like none we had ever seen. In a short period of time, a little over four days, we had over 700 men go through our aid station. Some were sick, some had trenchfoot, but the majority were battle casualties.

The men were fighting in a cold, wet, dark forest. They were under heavy mortar and artillery fire where a tree burst could kill or wound all below. Many of the attacks were at night, and wounded men might not be picked up until it became light.

One incident during this battle was a real tragedy. One company of the 18th was advancing through the dense woods and was using map coordinates as their only means to determine where they were. It was vital that they be in the proper area by a certain time because they were to be helped by a massive, time-on-target artillery barrage. This barrage would be delivered by as many as 200 big guns firing ten or so rounds as fast as they could and so timed they would all land in a very small area at the same time. Many of the shells were equipped with proximity fuses that had little radar detectors in the nose, and the shells would explode about ten feet from the ground. Part of the company got lost and was in the target area during the barrage. Many were killed, and the wounded men we received in the aid station were in a complete state of shock. A barrage like this would be like the end of the world.

A high percentage of the casualties in the four-day battle were new replacements. At first, a new man would be reluctant to drop to the cold wet

Sleeping quarters for Sgt. Towne at Cormolain, Normandy.

ground when a shell came over, especially if his clothes were dry, and he was not used to crawling in the mud. The new men would not think they must dig a hole and try to put a roof on it, if the stop was only for a short time. They wouldn't crawl on the ground or run when they should. And they did not have much time to learn. If a new replacement was not killed or wounded in the first two or three days, he had a much better chance of surviving.

Many times, during this action, replacements would come into the infantry units at night. Before they had a chance to even know what unit they were in, never mind to find a buddy they could depend on, they would be hit by shell fragments or small arms fire.

In the aid station, we had to make out tags on all the wounded to indicate what we had done to them. For example, we might have given them morphine or blood plasma. Further on in the chain of evacuation, they must have this information. We also had to record their names and organizations. During this period, when we asked the wounded men for the name of their unit, many would give a replacement depot number or admit they had no idea what unit they were with. They did not know they were in the 18th Infantry. Some had just come in at night a few hours before they were wounded. I felt sorry for these new men because not only were they hurt, but they were frightened and bewildered. The number of men going through the aid station with anxiety state increased. In some cases, there was outright desertion by a few individuals.

In one division, we heard it was the 9th Infantry Division, they had a man desert (Ernie Slovik). I believe he was the only man in the U.S. Army executed in World War II for desertion. We heard that his entire battalion was present when he was shot by a firing squad. The 9th Division was fighting in the Hürtgen forest at the time.

There was also a case of desertion in the 18th Infantry, but it was handled differently. During one of the real violent actions, one of the men kept running away. A master sergeant had a talk with the man to try to convince him to fight with the rest of the men. No combat unit can let a man shirk his duty in action or all discipline would disappear. The man said he was going to continue to run so the sergeant pulled out his pistol and shot the man dead. Later, the master sergeant came through the aid station to be sent back for a mental examination. The master sergeant returned in a few days with a clean bill of health and returned to his normal duties. That was the last I ever heard of the incident. It is hard for anyone who has not been exposed to long periods of hard combat to understand what this can do to even the best units.

During the battle in the Hürtgen forest, we had many men with anxiety state. We would get men in the aid station who would just sit there and shake. Others would be in a daze and have to be helped around. When given a place to sit, they would stay there, staring with vacant faces. In others, it would manifest itself in very different ways. One man came in and said he was blind and had to be led around. The doctors looked at his eyes and, after a few simple tests, concluded his eyes were all right. His mind had convinced him he was blind. We could not help him, so we sent him back to the field hospital for psychiatric help. Another was brought in because he could not talk. There did not seem to be anything wrong. We kept him overnight in the aid station, and during the night, he talked in his sleep. Yet, in the morning, he still could not talk. He was evacuated.

One man was sent back for a psychiatric examination. When I talked to him, he proudly showed me his collection of ears, which he had cut off dead German soldiers. He claimed he took them from the Germans he had killed. I later wondered if he had been with the 18th Infantry Regiment in Sicily when we had a unit of Goums fighting with the 18th. The Goums would go on patrol at night and quietly cut the throats of the Germans on outpost duty and bring back the ears of the men they had killed as proof of their work. Later, another man, who was collecting teeth from dead Germans, had to be sent to the rear for a psychiatric examination. One man, who I had seen taking German prisoners to the rear, was being sent back for an examination. He was suspected of deliberately shooting German prisoners. He always gave the excuse that they had tried to escape.

I often wondered if any of these men were permanently affected by their breakdowns. Or were they unstable in civilian life and this type of an experience just intensified the problem? Yet, in all this misery, most of the men stood up well. For example, one man, who had been slightly wounded, was helping three other men carry another wounded man on a litter when a shell came in and hit very close to them. The shell fragments killed the other four men. This man was still only slightly wounded and, when we got him in the aid station, he was quite cheerful. He was a rifleman who had been a gambler in New Orleans before he went into the Army and took things as they came. He had been wounded before and had been in the aid station four or five times over the years. His comment to me was, "Don't play blackjack with me. I am too lucky." Over the years, his main concern had been how to send his gambling winnings back to the States.

The great number of casualties made manpower a big problem. It forced the 18th Infantry to use its band members in combat, and several of them came through wounded during this battle.

On November 27, the German positions defending Langerwehe and the open area west of Düren were overrun, and the 18th had finally accomplished its mission. However, during the night of November 26-27, the Germans brought up a new unit, the 3d German Parachute Division, for a major attack. Because the high ground was now held by the 18th Infantry, our artillery could be accurately directed on the Germans. When they attacked, the Germans got caught in a huge artillery barrage, suffered large losses and surrendered in droves.

The 26th Infantry Regiment of the 1st Division did not fare as well in its battle with the German paratroopers. Two companies of the 2d Battalion had taken the German town of Merode, which was just outside of the forest on the plain of Cologne. They were cut off from the rest of the division when one of their supporting tanks was knocked out and blocked a narrow trail in the forest. This was their only supply road through the forest. The men held the town of Merode against heavy German attacks until their ammunition ran out. On December 1, any men that were still alive were taken prisoner.

December 1–7, 1944. Nothberg, Germany

We left Vicht at 1445 hours and traveled eight miles and arrived at 1500 hours. The station was set up and operating normally. The litter bearers and ambulances were with the infantry battalions. From this position, we could see many of the German (V-1) Buzz bombs going over. They could have been headed to England or one of the Dutch ports. Occasionally, one would malfunction and hit nearby. They made a tremendous noise when they exploded. We also saw the V-2 rockets slowly go up in the air and disappear. We never knew where they were headed, but we thought they were heading toward the port of Antwerp. The local civilians in the area (Germans) were now telling us that Hitler has a surprise Christmas present for us, and the increase in the activity of the V weapons is just the beginning.

On December 7, the 18th Combat Team was replaced by units of the 9th Infantry Division. The Hürtgen forest was one of the bloodiest battles in Europe and yet little is said about it. Perhaps the battle was a mistake. Two U.S. divisions were almost destroyed here, and two others were hurt badly. The furious German defense in the Hürtgen forest was to prevent the capture of the huge Rur (Roer) river dams located at nearby Schmidt. As long as the Germans held these dams, any penetration by U.S. forces to the plain of Cologne would put the Americans between the Rur and Rhine rivers. They then would be vulnerable to a German counterattack because, if the Rur dams were opened, the rush of water would swell the Rur river by up to 25 feet in depth and the width up to 2½ miles. Thus, any force caught in the plain of Cologne would be unable to be supplied, except by air, until the water subsided.

The reason I say that the battle may have been a mistake is because our objective in this battle was to cross the Rur river and yet no unit in the U.S. Army had the objective of capturing the Rur river dams. If we had succeeded in crossing the Rur, we would have been isolated when the Germans opened the Rur river sluice gates.

While the 1st Division had met its limited objectives in the battle of the Hürtgen forest, others had not been able to meet their objectives, and so the offensive was halted. The 1st Division suffered 3,400 casualties in two weeks of action in the Hürtgen forest. It was worse than D Day in Normandy. If you counted the loss of men from other reasons, such as trenchfoot, sickness and anxiety state, the total number lost was about 4,500 men. This was over 25 percent of the division strength.

Seventeen

Battle of the Bulge

December 8–16, 1944. Volkerich, Belgium

We left Nothberg, Germany, at 0900 hours and arrived at 1030 hours after traveling 28 miles. The roads and the weather were good, but the traffic was bad near the front lines because there was only one road available. Soon after we had left our position, we were held up at a crossroad, where the incoming units were crossing our exit road. Trucks, artillery, tanks and other types of vehicles were all jammed up and backed up for miles. I was glad that there were not any German planes in the area or we would have been in a lot of trouble.

We set up the aid station in a building in Volkerich but we did not expect to do much beyond sick call because this was to be a rest area. We checked clothing, equipment, supplies and vehicles. Showers were available. Because they were set up outside, the cold weather convinced me to take a fast shower.

Some of us were able to get passes to some nearby Belgian cities, and a few got passes to Paris. This was the first opportunity since we had left England, in early June, to go to a large town and buy anything. About all we could buy was something to eat and drink. Most of the men went to Liège, the nearest large Belgian city. In Liège, the Army had set up a place for the soldiers to sleep. Here, we could see a show and spend some money. Most of us had the greater portion of our pay sent home because we had few places to spend money. I was on a 24-hour pass to Liège when orders came for all 1st Division men to return to their units, so I did not have much of a chance to look at the sights of Liège.

The 1st Division was being replaced in the line a combat team at a time. As the last units pulled out of the line and into the rest area, the entire 1st Division was alerted to move on six hours' notice. On December 16, 1944, the Germans had launched a major counteroffensive against the U.S. forces in the Ardennes. This was a lightly held position in the center of the U.S. Army line between Monschaus and Echternach. The German objective was to cut off the Allied supply port of Antwerp and the communication center at Brussels. The major effort was to be made by the German 6th Panzer Army, consisting of four SS Panzer Divisions and five other divisions.

It was the German plan to have the 12th SS (Hitler's Elite Guard) Panzer Division spearhead the drive going through Bütgenbach toward Spa and Liège. To be successful, the 6th Panzer Army needed to control a minimum of five roads through the Ardennes. Three of these went over the Elsenborn ridge. Without these roads, the total plan could not succeed. One of the initial objectives was to capture the large supply dumps in the Liège, Verviers and Eupen area. The Germans would need these supplies, especially the gasoline, to continue their drive.

The weather was cold, cloudy and foggy. This limited the use of our huge air superiority, which might have stopped the German drive if it could have been used. On the night of December 16—actually, it was a little after midnight so it was the 17—the 26th Infantry Regimental Combat Team was sent to help the U.S. 99th Infantry Division hold its defensive positions at Bütgenbach, Belgium. This was an important road junction at a place called Camp Elsenborn on the vital Elsenborn ridge. It was at the northern flank of the German attack, where the Germans had broken through some of the 99th Division positions. The 26th Infantry Combat Team was ordered to contain the German effort.

Part of the 18th Infantry Regimental Combat Team was sent to Eupen to back up the 47th Infantry Regiment of the U.S. 9th Infantry Division. The remainder of the 18th was given the task of clearing out the 700 or so German paratroopers who had been dropped behind our lines in the area of the Malmedy-Eupen woods on the night of December 16-17. These paratroopers were a special unit, led by a Col. Von der Heydte, who were supposed to disrupt the movement of troops and cause confusion and any other damage they could manage. One effort that succeeded was to mix up road signs, so reinforcements got lost.

December 17–19, 1944. Nispert, Belgium

We left Volkerich at 1800 hours and traveled 11 miles and arrived at 1945 hours. Although the weather and roads were good, the traveling was slow due to the great amount of traffic leaving the area where we were headed. It seemed to us that all the other units in the U.S. Army were leaving the front lines and that the 18th Infantry Combat Team was the only one going toward the German breakthrough. There were rumors of Germans in U.S. uniforms in this area driving U.S. Army vehicles. Because of this, there were many roadblocks, which slowed the traffic.

When we got to Nispert, it was dark, and we set up the aid station. There was very little activity because most of the 18th Infantry was sweeping the woods south of Eupen for German parachutists and Germans dressed in American uniforms. The 18th Infantry captured or killed most of the

German paratroopers within 24 hours. They had been dropped in the wrong place and had been greatly dispersed. Thus, they were not a coordinated fighting force.

There was an amusing story going around that was supposed to be true. A specially trained German saboteur, equipped with an American uniform, dogtags and papers, was given the mission of slipping behind our lines to disrupt communications and supply routes. He got through the lines all right but, when he saw the array of talent lined up, waiting to entertain his countrymen, he changed his mind. He decided to give himself up, so he walked up to a fellow dressed in G.I. clothing and said, "I am a German soldier. I want to surrender."

In perfect German, he got his answer, "I am a member of the German sabotage group. You are a traitor."

The second German berated the surrendering man in German so loudly that several men of the 1st Division heard them, and both were bagged. Most of the Germans dressed in American uniforms were executed.

On December 18, the 18th Infantry took up positions in the line adjacent to the 26th Infantry Regiment. Throughout the day, the 12th Panzer Division tried to break through the 1st Division and capture the critical road junction. The attack was resumed on the 19th with additional German infantry and heavy artillery. Three tanks penetrated our lines. Two of them were knocked out by the infantry, and the third managed to escape. At midnight, the Germans attacked again, with ten tanks and a regiment of the 3d German Parachute Division Infantry but were repulsed. Later, they tried again, with right huge Panther tanks in the lead, but again they were driven back.

Most of this action was against the 2d Battalion of the 26th Infantry Regiment. They had recently lost two rifle companies at Merode in the Hürtgen forest. They were eager to get back at the Germans, and they did just that in this battle.

December 20–22, 1944. Ovifat, Belgium

We left at 1445 hours and traveled 15 miles, arriving at 1600 hours. The aid station was set up and in operation. This was a poor location and, except for an old shack, we did not have a proper place for working on casualties. It was quite cold, and we needed a warm area. There was a tremendous amount of German shelling that first night, and it was almost impossible to dig a hole in the frozen ground, so many of our men slept in the ruins of a nearby stone church. However, the stone floor was very cold, and no one got much sleep.

On the 21st, the Germans attacked again. This time, they had more infantry support as well as artillery and Nebelwerfers. They attacked with two battalions of armored infantry and 30 tanks. The Germans managed to break through the 26th Infantry line at one point with about 12 tanks and started firing point-blank at the infantrymen's holes and running over their holes with the tank treads. Our own tanks and tank destroyers managed to knock out 11 of them, and one got away.

By this time, the division had 12 battalions of artillery available to help beat back the fanatical SS troops. The Germans suffered huge losses. A count of dead German bodies showed 782 dead Germans. Forty-seven German tanks and tank destroyers were destroyed against our loss of three tanks and one tank destroyer and 250 casualties. This was the highwater mark of the German effort to break through at this critical area and seize the all-important three roads.

During the early days of the battle of the Bulge when it became known that the German plan was to go through the Elsenborn ridge at Bütgenbach, a high staff officer at Allied supreme headquarters was heard to say, "We are not worried about the Northern shoulder of the gap in our lines because the First Infantry Division is there."*

December 23–24, 1944. Elsenborn, Belgium

We left Ovifat at 1320 hours and traveled ½ mile to a new location, arriving at 1400 hours. The station was set up and operating. By December 23, the heavy German attacks in this area had stopped. They brought in infantry troops to hold the line while they moved what was left of their Panzer forces elsewhere. This meant that the major objective of their counteroffensive was lost, and they could only have a limited goal left.

On the morning of the 23d, we had good weather, and all the Allied planes were out for the first time in this battle. They were busy all day, bombing and strafing the German troops and positions. We could see the contrails of the big bombers overhead as they went to destroy the bridges and railroads to cut off the supplies to the German forces.

On the 24th, it was our third Christmas eve overseas, and this one was even worse than the one in North Africa, where it was wet and cold. Here, it was below freezing and very hard to keep warm.

December 25, 1944–January 12, 1945.
Elsenborn (2 miles south), Belgium

We left Elsenborn at 1400 hours and traveled two miles and arrived at 1415 hours. We set up the aid station and were in operation. This was a better

In Danger Forward *(1947), page 342.*

location because it was in a house. We could keep it warm by using a cook stove unit. We did have a good Christmas meal. We even had turkey and all the extras. Our dinner was warm, but many men were not able to get a warm meal.

News came in about the shooting of unarmed American prisoners by a unit of the German 1st Panzer Division at Malmédy. It seems that two of the men who were in the group that were shot and left for dead were 1st Division ambulance drivers. They had become lost from the 26th Infantry Regiment convoy and were captured by Kampfgruppe Peiper's Panzer force of about 4,000 soldiers. They were Pvts. Ray Anderson and Samuel Dobyns. They both dropped to the ground when the Germans fired on the unarmed group lined up in a field. Dobyns was shot four times, but Anderson was not hit. They managed to get away, and both lived. The ambulance drivers were probably members of Company C of the 1st Medical Battalion. This incident about the shooting of unarmed American soldiers made everyone angry. On December 28, a three-man German patrol tried to surrender to men of the 26th Infantry. Someone saw one German had a machine pistol behind his back. They were immediately shot by men of the 26th Infantry.

The activity here was now limited to heavy artillery duels and strong patrol activity. There were differing opinions in the high places of our command structure. Many U.S. commanders felt it was time to attack and cut off the Germans at the shoulders of the salient. However, the U.S. 1st Army was now under the command of the British general Montgomery, who was a very cautious general, and he did not want to attack. He even wanted us to give up the strategic Elsenborn ridge. The U.S. 1st Army commander convinced him not to do this.

In late December, real bad weather set in, and snow piled up and the temperature stayed below freezing.

January 13–27, 1945. Nidrum, Belgium

We left the last area at 1500 hours and traveled 1½ miles, arriving at 1530 hours. The station was set up in a house and in operation. On January 15, 1945, the division began the attack to close off the Bulge. The weather was so bad that the Germans did not believe we would attack, and so they were surprised.

It was surprising how many men would get wounded and go through our aid station and return to their units and then get wounded again. It got so that I would recognize many of them and greet them like old friends. One of them had a piece written about him in an 18th Infantry newsletter.

> It's getting to be a habit with S/Sgt. Max Bloom, Brooklyn, N.Y., a squad leader in K Company, 18th Infantry Regiment, who was awarded a sixth cluster to his Purple Heart Award.

Sgt. Bloom was first wounded in Sicily. He rejoined the regiment in England and was with it, up to Aachen, when he was slightly wounded. He was also injured at Allendorf. He left his company after being wounded on the famous Crucifix Hill and rejoined in the Hürtgen forest where he was wounded on two different occasions, but remained with G Company until they were out of the forest. At that point, he stopped some shrapnel from an 88-mm. shell and was evacuated in November. He rejoined the Fighting First in the middle of January and was in the second drive to the Siegfried Line. On the 24th Sgt. Bloom was grazed by shrapnel and added another cluster to his collection.

January 28–February 5, 1945. Schoppen, Belgium

The aid station, without the rest of the company, moved ten miles to Schoppen. The rest of the company would follow the next day.

The fighting in the Ardennes was much different from that in Africa, Sicily and even in France. Here, we had the bitter cold and much snow. Now that the combat team was on the offensive, the difficulties were more intense. Even things as mundane as digging a foxhole became a problem because the ground was frozen. The infantrymen would have to use dynamite to blast a hole. If a man got hit and nobody saw him, he could easily freeze to death, even if the wound was not too serious.

Our aid station was set up in a vacant house on the outskirts of the small village of Schoppen. The house was small but had a good level entrance that made it easy to load the ambulances. We cleared out three of the rooms to set up the aid station. I am somewhat ashamed of the way we cleaned out the rooms. We just opened the windows and doors and threw everything outside in the snow. Then, we brought in a gasoline heating unit from a cooking stove to heat the rooms. We needed a lot of space so that all the wounded men could be in a heated area. Many of them would be in shock and must be kept warm to survive. We also needed to keep the blood plasma warm. It was necessary to provide hot drinks for the wounded because we had to keep them in the aid station until an ambulance was full. The trip back to the clearing company was a treacherous trip for the ambulances in the snow, especially at night.

During one busy night, I was administering plasma to one wounded soldier. Another of our men was cutting the trousers off another infantryman, who had what looked like a shell fragment wound in the upper part of his right leg. As soon as the trouser was cut off, the blood spurted from the man's leg as if it was from a hose. The stream was so powerful that it hit the ceiling. We immediately applied a tourniquet on his leg, and one of the doctors tied off the femoral artery. Apparently, the blood had coagulated from the intense cold outside and, when he was brought inside the heated area, the blood thinned and broke the clot. We immediately started the man on blood plasma but, after a while, we could see it was not having much effect because the man was not pulling out of the deep shock. One of the doctors said he needed whole blood to survive. We did not carry whole blood, and it would take hours to get him to the nearest field hospital.

The doctor decided to try direct transfusions using our aid station men as donors. We all have our blood type on our dog tags so we could easily match the blood. I immediately set up and sterilized some large syringes and needles. We started by drawing blood from one of our men and injecting the blood in the wounded soldier. At first, the transfusion seemed to go well. However, after about half of the first syringe was transferred into the man, the blood coagulated in the syringe. We had to get another syringe filled from another donor. As we continued the transfusion, the coagulation of the blood made the process so time-consuming that the man died before we could get enough whole blood into his system.

The doctor who started the transfusions of whole blood had been getting flustered and red in the face and sweat was dripping from his forehead. When the man died, he was very upset. By this time, we had several wounded German soldiers in the aid station, and one of them, an SS soldier, was in deep shock. As I was preparing to give him plasma, the doctor who had been giving the whole blood to the wounded American said, "This German is the cause of this. Take him outside and let him die."

I had several of our men take him out of the room but, instead of putting him outside we put him in another heated room. When the medical officer left, we brought the German soldier back and started to give him blood plasma, but he also died.

On February 5, a wide breach was made through the Siegfried line north of Hollerith, and the 1st Division was relieved by the 99th Infantry Division. During the 21 days of continuous attacks, the division had taken over 2,000 prisoners and had killed and wounded many more.

February 6, 1945. Hunningen, Belgium

We left Schoppen at 1400 hours and traveled eight miles, arriving at 1600 hours. The station was set up and in operation. Although the 18th Infantry Combat Team was no longer fighting in this area, we were still getting casualties from the previous action. Patrols were scouring the area to find wounded men because it had been snowing and the snow could have covered them.

We received two infantrymen in the aid station who had been out in a ditch, wounded, and had been covered with snow for at least 24 hours. They were both in deep shock and, after much difficulty, we finally got the plasma

needles into their veins (the veins were sunken and very small). They responded to the plasma, and we could see the color coming back into their gray
faces as the plasma bottles drained. We gave each of them a second bottle of
plasma in a heated ambulance and took the two men directly to a field hospital that had moved closer. Because the action in this area was over, Sgt.
McFarland and I went with the wounded men to make sure nothing went
wrong while they were traveling to the hospital. When the ambulance got to
the field hospital, two Army nurses, dressed in fatigues, came out of the hospital tent and took charge of the two men. The wounded men, plasma bottles still attached, were carried into the heated tent to the operating room.
They immediately started to work on them. This time, both men lived.

February 7–8, 1945. Vieuxville
(½ mile west), Belgium

   We left at 1115 and traveled 43 miles, arriving at 1500 hours. The station
was set up but there would not be much activity as the 18th Infantry Combat Team was not in action.

Eighteen

Crossing the Rhine

February 9–26, 1945. Vicht, Germany

We left Vieuxville, Belgium, at 1315 hours and traveled 60 miles by truck and arrived at Vicht at 1700 hours. The aid station was set up but, as this was a quiet area, we did not expect much activity. The 18th Infantry Combat Team was now on the edge of the Roer/Rur river. We were very close to where we were just before the battle of the Bulge and were not far from the German city of Düren. The German forces were on the other side of the river.

The Germans had fought hard in the Hürtgen forest so they could control the Rur River dams. After they retreated across the river, they destroyed all the bridges over the Rur river and then blew up the Rur river dams. The river had flooded and was impassable until the water subsided. They did this to give themselves time to set up new defenses on the east side of the river.

I still think our that attack through the Hürtgen forest was a costly error of the Allied high command. Even if we had been able to cross the Rur river when we had been here a few months previous, we would have been cut off when the Germans opened the Rur river dams and released the water from the Rur reservoirs. The bloody battle of the Hürtgen forest gained nothing.

The 18th Infantry Combat Team had to wait about three weeks for the river to subside. The long wait gave us time to clean up. Showers and clean clothes were available. We also had time to check our equipment, supplies and vehicles. This time, there were no interruptions, and there was time for recreation. A few men, who had married English girls, were able to get furloughs to England, and a few who had not been able to get passes before the battle of the Bulge were able to get passes to Paris.

The weather was starting to get warmer and somewhat pleasant. One very warm day, I sat out in the sun for several hours. Later that night, I developed a real sunburn. It was hard to believe that, in February, I could get a sunburn. I never got a sunburn before. Not even in North Africa. I couldn't figure out why until I realized that I had been in the aid station continually for the past four months. The aid station had always been set up in houses because of the cold weather. In the almost five years I had been in the Army,

I had never been inside as much as in the past four months. Most of the time, I had lived outside but, during the past winter, I had a prison pallor.

By February 25, the Rur river had subsided, and the 1st Division Combat Teams crossed the river on the U.S. 8th Infantry Division's pontoon bridges, which were downstream from our position. We surprised the Germans by attacking the defenders from their rear. The 1st Division then established its own bridgeheads over the Rur river.

In the initial attack over the Rur, I went with part of the aid station group and litter bearers over the Roer via a narrow footbridge. The 1st Division then went on the attack toward the Rhine river, heading between the German cities of Cologne and Bonn. These attacks on the plain of Cologne were usually at night. The 1st Division Combat Teams liked to attack at night and always caught the Germans by surprise. The Germans would reorganize their positions at night, and these attacks kept them off-balance.

February 27, 1945. Lendersdorf, Germany

After the infantry had secured another bridgehead and the 1st Division Engineers had erected a pontoon bridge, the remainder of the aid station and the ambulance platoon crossed the Rur river on the pontoon bridge. They left at 1330 hours and traveled 19 miles and joined us at the temporary aid station at 1440 hours. The complete aid station was set up and in operation.

February 28–March 1, 1945.
Girbelsrath, Germany

The complete aid station and the ambulance platoon left Lendersdorf at 1330 hours and traveled seven miles, arriving at 1415 hours. During this move, we went through the city of Düren. Düren was an important road and rail junction west of Cologne and had been the target of many Allied bombing raids. The city was demolished.

I stood on the running board of our ¾-ton truck and could see over the entire city. It was completely leveled. The roads had to be bulldozed to clear a passageway through the rubble. It was like going through a snow-plowed street.

When we got to Girbelsrath, we set up the aid station and proceeded to evacuate the wounded. The German resistance was not as heavy as it was prior to the battle of the Bulge because they had suffered many casualties and were not able to replace them. The advance of the Russian army into Germany on their eastern front had also made it difficult for them to supply reinforcements

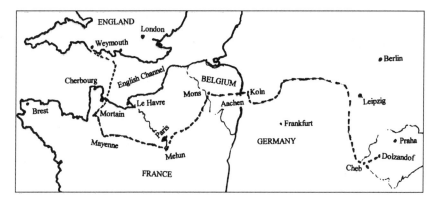

The route of the 18th RCT in Europe from June 6, 1944 to May 23, 1945.

to this sector. The Germans did not have large organized units to defend this area and were using parts of larger units and many anti-aircraft units as ground troops.

March 2–6, 1945. Norvenich, Germany

We left Girbelsrath at 1230 hours and traveled four miles, arriving at 1300 hours. The station was set up and, as there was more resistance, we had more casualties, including one of our own company. On March 2, Pvt. Harold R. Porter was wounded in action with a shell fragment in his left thigh and evacuated.

March 7, 1945, Heimersheim, Germany.

The aid station and ambulance platoon left Norvenich at 1700 hours and traveled nine miles, arriving at 1830 hours. We set up the aid station and were operating normally. The 18th Infantry had cleared the town of Ollekover and was now fighting in the outskirts of the Rhine city of Bonn.

March 8, 1945. Bonn, Germany

The aid station and ambulance platoon moved into the city of Bonn in late afternoon. We set up the aid station in one of the University of Bonn's buildings and proceeded to collect wounded and evacuate the casualties. The university was at a good location near the center of Bonn and was surrounded by a park, or perhaps it was the campus. It was not very far from the Rhine river.

The 18th Infantry tried to capture the large bridge across the Rhine but the German engineers had mined it and blew the bridge later that evening. After the bridge was blown, the German troops on our side of the river surrendered and, except for isolated cases, the battle for Bonn was over.

The 634th Tank Destroyer Battalion, which was attached to the 18th Infantry Combat Team, sunk a German naval vessel in this action. When they got up to the bank of the Rhine, they noticed a German vessel flashing signals to the other side and commenced firing on it. They saw German soldiers swimming from it when it was sinking. It is rare to have a tank destroyer engage in a naval action.

We saw many civilians in Bonn. Either they did not believe the city was going to be captured or they felt the war was lost and they might as well stay there.

March 9–15, 1945. Duisdorf, Germany

In the morning, I had a chance to explore the university buildings and found that, although it was an old university, it was a well-equipped school, at least in the science and chemistry buildings. The only damage was in the chemistry analytical balance room, where someone had knocked all of the analytical balances off the tables, and they were all broken. It looked as if a rifleman had walked down the rows of balances, and using his rifle, had knocked them all off. They probably made a lot of noise (breaking glass) when they fell. After many years in combat, you have different ideas of amusement.

Later in the day, the aid station and ambulance platoon rejoined the rest of the company and set up the aid station in Duisdorf. The only duty in this area was for the combat team to consolidate and hold the positions.

Some of our men found a wine warehouse under the street where we had our aid station. They brought up cases of wines. While the division waited for new orders, we had a chance to sample some vintage Rhine wines as a gift of the German government. The wine was excellent but a few of us were not aware of how potent some Rhine wines were. There were quite a few headaches the next day. At least, we had aspirin tablets to help with the hangovers.

We now knew that the 9th Armored Division, on our right flank, had captured an intact railroad bridge (Hindenburg bridge) over the Rhine at Remagen on March 7. We expected we would soon be across the Rhine the easy way (over a captured bridge).

The 1st Division was relieved in its position by the U.S. 8th Infantry Division on March 15.

March 16–19, 1945. Rheinbreitbach, Germany

We left Duisdorf at 0315 hours on May 16. The weather was foggy and, of course, it was very dark at three in the morning. We moved slowly in the dark. After a long drive, the convoy stopped and, as it started to get light, I saw the large railroad bridge that still spanned the Rhine. The Hindenburg bridge was still being used to take the troops to the other side of the river. However, we crossed the Rhine river at 0540 hours on a pontoon bridge a little upstream from the Remagen railroad bridge. There was a lot of men and equipment to go across so more bridges were needed. Also, the Hindenburg bridge had been damaged by heavy German shell fire and it might not stay intact. There were two pontoon bridges in operation, and the U.S. Navy had brought in some large landing craft to help in moving supplies over the river.

We traveled a total of 28 miles from Duisdorf and set up the aid station in a large house overlooking the Rhine river in the town of Rheinbreitbach. It was a beautiful house and nicely decorated. It had a tremendous view as it was located on a high hill overlooking the Rhine river. It looked like a castle and perhaps it had been a copy of one, although inside it was relatively modern. It had belonged to a well-known German author named Rudolf Herzog. He had died several years ago, and his widow was still living in the house. She told us to make ourselves at home in the house. We did just that. Some men played chess with a hand-carved ivory chess set that was in the study. I noticed when we left that the chess set was gone. Perhaps she took it or perhaps one of our men took it. Everyone felt the war would soon be over, and souvenir collecting was rampant.

The Germans were trying to knock out the bridges and were shelling the whole area. Some guns must have been of very large caliber from the sounds they made when they hit. They seemed to be firing right over the house.

On March 17, the Remagen railroad bridge, after being hit often, collapsed. There had been about 200 U.S. Army engineers working on it at the time, and about 20 were killed when the bridge fell into the river. The loss of the bridge did not affect the supply of ammunition, food or gasoline. The other pontoon bridges and the Navy boats were ample to take care of all the needed supplies.

On the 17th, the 18th Combat Team went on the offensive to expand the bridgehead. However, the attacks were limited. Because of political reasons, the Remagen bridgehead could only be expanded 1,000 yards per day. British General Montgomery had priority for men and supplies for his forthcoming attack across the Rhine north of Cologne.

Nineteen

Ruhr Pocket

March 20–21, 1945. Honnef, Germany

We left Rheinbreitbach at 1230 hours, traveled five miles and arrived at Honnef at 1315 hours. The aid station was set up and operating. The action was now severe as the Germans were bringing in more troops to try to contain the bridgehead. By the 21st, the Germans had begun a series of counterattacks, but they were broken up. Their artillery was quite intense, and they had some large-caliber guns that were very troublesome.

For the first time in the war, we had some wounded black soldiers go through our aid station. Up until a few weeks ago, there had been no black soldiers in the 18th Infantry and perhaps in the entire 1st Division. There was now one platoon in B Company of the 18th Infantry. They had been in a firefight and performed well. Several men had been wounded. Before this incident, I had not realized there were not any black soldiers in the 18th Infantry Regiment. I had never thought about it. I did know that there were many black soldiers in the European Theater of Operations but most of them were in the Quartermaster Corps. A good part of the Red Ball Express drivers seemed black. Besides the increase in the number of 18th Infantry Regiment casualties, we had two of our own men wounded on March 21: Pfc. Denver C. Barker (shell fragment wound, right leg) and Pfc. Charles H. Evens (shell fragment wound, right thigh). Both were evacuated.

March 22, 1945. Boseroth, Germany

We left Honnef at 1250 hours and traveled six miles, arriving at 1350 hours. The aid station was set up and in operation. This move was to get into a better position to support an attack by the 18th Infantry.

March 23, 1945. Oberpleis, Germany

We left Boseroth at 1215 hours and traveled a quarter mile, arriving at 1230 hours. We set up the aid station in a building near the center of the town.

It looked like an office of the Gestapo had been located in the building because of the furnishings and the pictures in the offices.

Late in the evening, the 18th Combat Team captured the high ground and the town of Wellesburg. On March 23, two more of our company were wounded: Pvt. Leo Guzik (shell fragment wound, left leg with a possible fracture) and Pvt. Howard L. Smith (shell fragment wound, left arm and left side of chest, penetrating). Most of our wounded have been the new replacements. We are not quite sure why because they are always with many older men.

On March 23, the U.S. 3d Army crossed the Rhine river south of us. On the 24th, the British forces under Montgomery crossed the Rhine to the north of us. This allowed the 1st Army commander to release the U.S. divisions in the Remagen bridgehead from the 1,000-yards-per-day restriction on advances.

The 1st Division prepared to go on a real attack. Also, it was obvious that the Germans were bringing in more troops and were planning a large, powerful counterattack.

March 24–25, 1945. Oberpleis, Germany

On the 24th, there were 14 German counterattacks, and enemy mortar, artillery and rocket fire was intense. More than 5,000 rounds hit the division area. Our artillery responded, and our fighter bombers were called in to help.

Our intelligence people told us that the entire German 130th Panzer Lehr Division was now moving into the area and was preparing to attack. However, we were also preparing to attack. The 3d Armored Division was lined up on the road next to our aid station ready for the 1st Division to break through the German lines. Most units of the 1st Division went on the attack on the night of the 24th (the usual night attacks). Again, the attack caught the Germans by surprise as they were getting ready for their large counterattack.

However, in the battle for a small town called Uckerath, the 2d Battalion of the 18th Infantry Combat Team made a daylight attack. Uckerath, a small town east of the Rhine river, was the place that our high command had decided would be a logical spot to make an armored breakthrough. It was to be a daylight attack because a delay would hinder the success of the attack. This made it more difficult for the infantry because they would be easier to spot and would not have the element of surprise.

It was a typical infantry attack against a fanatical German resistance. The enemy had access to reserve troops and supplies in the nearby town of Huehle. The German defense line was set up in a circle surrounding Uckerath and was supported by tanks. Their artillery and small arms covered every approach.

The attack by our infantry was to be across open terrain, and it would be difficult, if not impossible, not to have very heavy casualties. Supported by heavy artillery fire, the 18th infantrymen went forward. A platoon of F Company, under 1st Lt. Navotney, swung to the left and cut the German supply route from Huehle by securing a road junction on the edge of Uckerath. Meanwhile, F and E Companies were advancing slowly from the front. G Company came in from the north with tanks and smashed through the first German defenses.

Once we were inside the town, the Germans fought fanatically and would sacrifice many men just to get one American. It was a fierce battle, and the 18th Infantry Combat Team came under intense artillery, rocket and mortar fire. By nightfall, after a 12-hour battle, they had knocked the Germans out of this strategic and heavily defended town.

Now that Uckerath was completely in American hands and the 18th had secured the important road junction, the 3d Armored Division's Combat Command A roared through the gap for the race to encircle the Ruhr. The importance of this breakout was similar to the one near St. Lô in France, which allowed our armored divisions to encircle the German army in Normandy. Yet, far as I can determine, it has never been mentioned in the news media. The Ruhr valley was the industrial heart of Germany. There were three German armies in the Ruhr area along with 100,000 additional German anti-aircraft troops.

For hours, the 3d Armored Division's tanks rumbled past our aid station and through Uckerath. The riflemen from the 18th Infantry dug in to get a well-deserved night's sleep. In this action, on the 24th, our company suffered some additional casualties: Pvt. George P. Propard Jr. (shell fragment wound, left cheek; abrasions, right leg; evacuated) and Pvt. Owen M. McGinty (lacerated wound, left hand; remained on duty).

During this attack, G Company of the 2d Battalion of the 18th Infantry picked out a large house on the outskirts of Uckerath for a command post. When the company commander and his men entered the house, they found the place in an uproar. Countless civilians were screaming, laughing and crying. The company commander had no time to bother with civilians. He had the CP group set up radio and telephone communications, and the attack continued. Later, when the town was secure and the battle was over, the company commander made a tour of the command post and found it still in a state of bedlam. After talking to an English-speaking civilian, he found that the building was an insane asylum, housing 75 inmates. When the German artillery let up, the inmates were evacuated.

I picked up two souvenirs at the Gestapo headquarters, where we had our aid station. I found an SS dress dagger that the SS men must have worn at special events. It was about 12 inches long and came with a metal sheath. Imprinted on the blade was "Deutschland über Alles." Along with this, I found a P-38 pistol. This was a Luger pistol and was considered a prize souvenir.

March 26–27, 1945. Mendt, Germany

We left Oberpleis at 1415 hours and traveled nine miles. The aid station was set up and in operation. The battle of March 24-25 had been the climax of the action around the Remagen bridgehead because the Germans had committed their major units. During the past eight-day period, the division had destroyed more than 50 tanks and self-propelled guns and five German divisions. These were the 9th Panzer, the 130th Panzer, the 3d Panzer Grenadiers, the 62d Infantry and the 363d Infantry Divisions.

The 18th Infantry was now moving north, mopping up after the 3d Armored Division and forming a blocking force to prevent the Germans caught in this big pocket from escaping. There were few casualties because there was no real coordinated German action. Units of the 8th Infantry Division relieved the 18th Infantry on the 27th of March. As the 3d Armored Division advanced to close the trap, we followed to prevent the Germans from breaking out. Then, other U.S. Army units would take over our area, and the combat team would move on to follow the 3d Armored Division.

March 28, 1945. Weitefeld, Germany

We left Mendt at 1415 hours and traveled 32 miles, arriving at 1800 hours. The aid station was set up and in operation.

March 29–31, 1945. Burbach, Germany

We left Weitefeld at 1745 hours and traveled 14 miles, arriving at 1900 hours. The aid station was set up and in operation. We were now operating a little bit like the way we went through France and Belgium last summer. We were always on the move. One big difference was that we were in the enemy's country. The Germans were fighting to defend their own country, and so the fighting was constant, although some German units were apathetic and didn't fight well.

April 1–6, 1945. Leiberg, Germany

The 1st Division was ordered to prevent all enemy movement from the west and southwest to break out of the "Rose Pocket." This pocket was formed by the 3d Armored Division meeting with the 2d Armored Division of the U.S. 9th Army at Lippstadt, near Paderborn.

We left Burbach at 1540 hours and traveled almost all night in the long, blacked-out convoy of the 18th Infantry Combat Team. It was a wild night. Any time, we could expect to meet German units trying to break out of the huge trap in the Ruhr valley.

Gen. Rose, the commander of the 3d Armored Division, was killed this night in such an action near Paderborn. A group of German SS tank units tried to break through our lines to help the trapped German armies break out. The SS group was thrown back, and they retreated into the Hartz mountains.

We traveled 111 miles that night and arrived at 0200 hours. The aid station was set up and operating normally. We set up in a school and had plenty of room. We did have a little problem because the litter-bearer platoon decided to sleep in the chemistry laboratory. In the dark, they knocked over some large reagent bottles. They broke and caused fumes to go through the school. Some men had to be treated for smoke inhalation, and many decided to sleep outside.

April 7–8, 1945. Dalhausen, Germany

We left Leiberg at 1800 hours and traveled 39 miles, arriving at 2030 hours. The division was relieved by the 8th Division, and on April 8, was ordered to cross the Weser river and push on to clear the German army units in the Hartz mountains.

Eighteen U.S. divisions were now mopping up the encircled Germans in the Ruhr pocket and, on April 18, they surrendered. More than 325,000 German soldiers were taken prisoner in this pocket. This was the largest envelopment in the entire war.

Twenty

To the Elbe

April 9, 1945. Polier, Germany

We left Dalhausen at 1745 hours and crossed the Weser river over a pontoon bridge at 1815 hours. After traveling a total of 15 miles, we came to Polier. The aid station was set up and operating normally.

This area, the Weser-Hartz mountains, was the central training ground for the German Army and a high percentage of the troops opposing us were from training and replacement units. Some regular German army units were also in the area, so it was a mix of well-trained and trainees, and they were not very well organized to fight as a coordinated force. However, the terrain was ideal for defense. There were thick woods and, in places, it was quite mountainous. The Germans had about 100,000 troops in the area.

The 18th Infantry Combat Team's mission was to clear its assigned area of German soldiers. It was attacking at Northeim, Weibrechsh, Subheim, Hillerse, Lagershausen and Fredelsloh.

April 10, 1945. Northeim, Germany

The 18th Infantry captured Northeim early in the day. We left Polier at 1415 hours and traveled 33 miles, arriving at Northeim at 1800 hours. The aid station was set up and operating as usual.

Nearby was a railhead, and we saw many railroad cars with V-2 rockets loaded on them. The rockets were manufactured near here, and they were ready to ship to launching sites. However, the German transportation system was practically destroyed, and the rail cars never moved. It was a good thing the Germans did not have the V-1 and V-2 rockets and jet aircraft earlier in the war because they could have caused us a great deal of trouble and the war could have lasted a lot longer.

April 11, 1945. Lindau, Germany

German resistance was getting a little stronger as the division got close to some German army tank repair depots. Five German tanks were knocked out in the action today.

We left Northeim at 1300 hours and traveled eight miles, arriving at 1345 hours. This was a recreational ski area, and I could see the ski lodges on the mountain slopes. It was beautiful country and I imagine that, in the winter with snow on the ground, it could be breathtaking.

We set up the aid station in a ski lodge. The aid station was set up in the lobby, and the rest of the men slept in the guest rooms. Everyone decided we would take any comfort we could find because we were in the middle of enemy territory. The trouble was that we did not stay a long enough to enjoy the comfort.

April 12–14, 1945. Schwiegershausen, Germany

We left Lindau at 1245 hours and traveled six miles, arriving at 1330 hours. We set up the aid station and proceeded to evacuate casualties.

The 18th Infantry encountered many roadblocks and had to eliminate small groups of Germans who had tanks and self-propelled guns. Again ,there were no coordinated enemy attacks, and we suffered few casualties.

There were many German army supply depots in this area. Because everyone could sense that the German army was beginning to fall apart, all of the U.S. soldiers were picking up souvenirs.

One day, we had five men come into the aid station with gunshot wounds in the hands. The wounds were not serious because they were from very small caliber bullets. The men were all from the same infantry company, and they had to be evacuated to a field hospital. This was a serious problem because replacements were hard to obtain. The company commander of the rifle company investigated and discovered that the men had found a supply of small automatic pistols. Apparently, they were the type issued to German army nurses.

The guns were so small that they were difficult for the infantrymen to handle. When the men were loading the weapons, they shot themselves. The company commander decided to call the entire company together and warn everyone to be careful and leave these guns alone. While he was showing the men how dangerous it was to handle the little gun, it went off, and the bullet went through his hand. He was one angry and mortified company commander when he came into our aid station a short time later.

Over the years, I have seen about 15 infantrymen who have accidentally shot themselves. These were men who have their guns with them always. The worst case was a man who had his rifle loaded and the safety off. This man had the habit of placing the stock of his rifle on the ground and clasping his hands over the muzzle and laying his chin on his hands. He must have done something to cause the rifle to fire, and the bullet went through his hands and head, killing him instantly.

On April 12, the 1st Battalion of the 18th Infantry joined the 3d Armored Division's Combat Command A in a race from Northeim to the Elbe river city of Dessau. At first, they bypassed the villages and towns but, when the tank-riding riflemen came within 15 miles of Dessau, they had a fight on their hands.

The firefights in the preceding towns had been the usual pitched battles between riflemen and machine gunners and, usually, the Germans took off after a determined defense. The fight for Dessau was the big battle. Pre-battle reconnaissance and prisoner reports indicated that a determined defense was setup in the historical city. It was even rumored that Hitler ordered the defenders to fight to the last man. The real fight came after the 1st Battalion had cleaned up its assigned sector of Dessau. It came in a small village 2,000 yards beyond Dessau along the Elbe river, where a battalion of German OCS candidates fought fanatically to stem the American advance. From noon to midnight, the battle went on, but the rifle companies moved forward. Finally, the 18th prevailed and cleared them out to the Elbe. The U.S. forces in this sector were to wait here for the Russian army to come up to the other side of the Elbe.

On April 13, we heard that President Roosevelt had died. I wondered if this would have any effect on the war in Europe but, after thinking it over, I did not think it would. The Germans were in no position to do much more fighting. It could have a bearing on the fighting in the Pacific, where the fighting could last a lot longer. I felt that most of us who had been in the Army a long time would not have to go to the Pacific. However, I was a little concerned when I found out that my MOS (military occupation specialty) number was considered essential. I might have trouble getting out with the first group to get discharged from the Army.

April 15–16, 1945. Sieber, Germany

We left Schwiegershausen at 1750 hours and traveled 16 miles, arriving at 1850 hours. We set up the aid station as usual. New units of the German army kept coming into the area as they tried to get away from other U.S. divisions. Elements of the German 5th Parachute Division were now being captured.

We had an infantryman come into the aid station who had hurt himself trying to blow open a safe in a German bank with a bazooka. He was unsuccessful in opening the safe. I do not think he was after German money because that was probably worthless. He probably wanted to see if it could be done and perhaps he could find a souvenir.

I picked up a souvenir in a nearby German army supply base. It was a Lietz 35-mm slide projector that had been used in a German army office. I still have it. I also picked up a 16-mm sound movie projector, but I could not get the sound to work properly and, anyway, it was too heavy so I discarded it.

Another unit in the U.S. Army captured a warehouse full of new Leica cameras and passed them around. There were now quite a few new Leicas being traded.

One tank driver, who knew the value of the element mercury, came across a supply and filled up one of his gasoline tanks with the liquid metal. He thought he could sell it to someone. He found that it was so heavy that it was troublesome so he drained it out in a ditch at the side of the road. The men were doing many strange things.

April 17–19, 1945. Stiege, Germany

We left Sieber at 0845 hours and, on the way, we came out of the southeast part of the Hartz mountains. As we broke out of the thick woods, I could see we were at the end of the mountainous territory, and the plains that led to the Elbe and Berlin stretched out below. The town of Nordhausen was at the base of the hill below us. At this time, there was a huge fire blazing in what seemed to be oil storage tanks, and black smoke partly obscured the town. We went down the mountain and drove through the outskirts of Nordhausen, which was an old medieval town. We then went in a northerly direction toward Thale, where the 18th Combat Team was now mopping up the last resistance in this sector. After a 59-mile drive, we arrived at Stiege at 1220 hours. The aid station was set up and in operation.

The bag of prisoners was increasing, and the 18th captured about 8,000 German soldiers near Thale, which was captured on April 19th.

A Russian soldier who had been captured by the Germans and now was free came into the aid station to get information as to what he should do to get back to Russia. We could only send him back to division headquarters. However, I was amazed that he knew all about the proposed formation of the United Nations and even was familiar with the meetings going on in the United States regarding the U.N. He was more knowledgeable than we were on the U.N. and was very enthusiastic about it.

April 20–23, 1945. Thale, Germany

We left Stiege at 1715 hours. We traveled 14 miles and arrived at 1915 hours. The aid station was set up as usual.

The next day, we found that Nordhausen was the site of a Nazi concentration camp. Several of our doctors went back to inspect the camp. When they came back later in the day, they were quite shaken by the atrocities that the Nazis had committed at the death camp. It was hard to believe that civilized people could exterminate millions of defenseless people.

The German army in this area was disorganized. Many soldiers believed the war was over and were surrendering. On April 21, one of our sergeants and a corporal captured eight German soldiers. They were one major general, one major, four lieutenants and two privates.

The aid station was again located near another German army supply depot. We picked up a shortwave radio that could reach the States and a mobile generator (220 volts) that would power the radio and give us electric lights. The generator was on a trailer, and we hitched it behind our truck. We actually picked up two generators. The other was a small portable one. The large one gave us some trouble at first because it was running in reverse, but we finally got it running properly. It was supposed to run on kerosene but we did not have any kerosene so we ran it on gasoline. This probably would wear it out fast, but we did not expect to keep it very long.

The infantrymen were also collecting all kinds of German army equipment, trucks and even Volkswagens. The original Volkswagen was supposed to be a "people's car" made for the average German. They were four door convertibles. When the war started, they were used by the German army. The 18th Infantry Combat Team convoy was beginning to look like a gypsy outfit.

By now, all German resistance in front of the division had collapsed ,and the U.S. 1st and 9th Armies had stopped at the Elbe river to wait for the Russian army.

On April 22, the 1st Infantry Division positions were taken over by the U.S. 8th Division, and the 1st Division was transferred from the U.S. 1st Army to the V Army Corps of the U.S. 3d Army. We were immediately ordered to move a long way south to Czechoslovakia, where the U.S. Army was still on the offensive against the Germans. I think our high command wanted to end the war as soon as possible and felt that a veteran division would be more efficient than an inexperienced one and suffer fewer casualties. However, we felt it was unfair for us to always be on the attack. We also wondered if we would have to fight to take the so-called Redoubt. This was supposed to be the fortress area in the Thuringian forest near Berchtesgaden.

It was rumored that the Nazi party was planning to hold out until it could get its underground organized for a counterattack and be in a better position to negotiate on peace terms. There were supposed to be large quantities of weapons and supplies stored there. We were told that they even had aircraft factories there. There had been many rumors about this in the last few weeks. The real fanatical Nazis were supposed to be gathering there for the last big battle.

Twenty-one

The Last Battle

April 24–27, 1945. Ahlsdorf, Germany

We left Thale at 1330 hours and traveled 50 miles, arriving at 1530 hours. The traveling was much easier because we were able to go on excellent highways. In spite of the large convoy, we made good time. This time, we set up the aid station in an elementary school. There wasn't any electric power in the town so we cut the power line at the school's service entrance and attached our newly obtained German army generator (the large one on the trailer) to the school circuit. It worked fine, except all the electric bulbs seemed very bright. In a short time, all the bulbs burned out. We discovered that this part of Germany uses 110 volts as the standard electrical voltage. This is different from the rest of the Germany, which has 220 volts as the standard voltage.

Our generator had a 220-volt output so we had overloaded the bulbs. We were unable to change the output of the generator, but we did have some 220-volt bulbs with us. So, we were able to continue to use our new modern convenience of electric lights. The generator output was 50 cycles, which meant we could not use any American-made radios because all of the U.S. radios ran on 60 cycles. We had to use our German army radios.

We were now close to Leipzig and not very far from Berlin. The 1st Battalion of the 18th Infantry and Combat Command A of the 3d Armored Division had been fighting some miles east of the rest of us, and we were now close to them. They were at Dessau on the west bank of the Elbe, about 45 miles from Berlin. The 1st Battalion was relieved by another infantry unit so it could go with the rest of the combat team to Czechoslovakia. The 3d Armored Division was not going with us.

April 28–30, 1945. Arzberg, Germany

We left Ahlsdorf at 1240 hours and traveled south on an autobahn on the west side of Leipzig. The autobahn was in good condition, and all the bridges were standing so the traveling was comfortable. There were no hostilities of any type, but we still traveled slowly because of the large convoy of Army vehicles on the road. The convoy left the autobahn near the old town of Hof and proceeded toward the Czechoslovakian border. We arrived at Arzberg at 2130 hours after having traveled 157 miles. We spent the rest of the night there near the Czechoslovakian border. It is about 30 miles north of Bayreuth and 60 miles north of Nürnberg.

The aid station was set up and in operation. This time, we set up in a German bierhaus (pub). It was small but very nice. All around the walls, there were shelves that held beer steins with the owners' names on them. They must come in and use their individual steins. Most of the steins had covers on them. We managed to open a keg of the beer, and we used other people's steins. The beer was good. The pub owner was nowhere to be found.

In a move like this, we had very little to do because the 18th Infantry was not in contact with the enemy. Everyone's spirits were high because we were sure the war would soon be over.

May 1–5, 1945. Cheb (Eger), Czechoslovakia

We left Arzberg at 1830 hours and traveled ten miles, arriving at 1930 hours. I found it interesting and somewhat confusing that the cities on the border of Germany and Czechoslovakia—and even well inside the countries—would have two names. One would be German and the other Czechoslovakian. It made it difficult when I was trying to trace our routes with new maps after the war. The names had changed back to the original names and did not use the ones the Germans had assigned. One of the division objectives in Czechoslovakia was Karlsbad, but now it is not listed by that name but rather as Karlovy Vary. So we were now in Cheb (Eger).

Cheb was a fairly large place, and we set up the aid station in a building on the outskirts. Near the aid station were some apartment buildings, and a little farther away, there were factories and warehouses. The factories were not in operation, and it seemed as if all the men had left or were hiding. There were plenty of women and children living in the apartment buildings so the authorities must not have ordered the people to evacuate the area.

Some women in the apartment buildings came over and asked for food, so the local distribution system must have broken down. They were especially concerned about fresh fruit, oranges in particular, for their children. We were now obtaining excellent rations and did have oranges, so we gave some to the children. They were very grateful and enjoyed the candy we gave them.

We heard about the death of Adolf Hitler, and we were now sure the war would soon be over in Europe. Everyone was in high spirits and was doing foolish things. Someone had discovered a nearby warehouse full of glass chimneys used in oil lanterns. The glass chimneys were piled on shelves about

15 feet high. A group went in the warehouse and started to throw rocks to see how much noise they could make. The noise was loud but the destruction foolish. Who cared?

Apparently, there was a question whether the U.S. Army would attack into Czechoslovakia. We waited for several days for orders. Finally, on May 5, the 1st Division, with attached Combat Command B of the 9th Armored Division, commenced the attack on the German positions in the direction of Karlsbad. The aid station and the ambulance platoon moved to a position in the woods near the infantry battalions, and the rest of the company remained in Cheb.

The division's attack was on a 48-kilometer-wide front against a mixture of German units under the command of Gen. Benicke. The force was called Division Benicke. The German army was now in real bad shape because they lacked any well-organized units. However, one of these groups turned out to be some of the best troops found in Czechoslovakia because they were from an officer candidate school at Milowitz. (This was a large military training center.) They gave the 18th Infantry some trouble, but the enemy was soon in retreat. By the next day, there had been a general advance of 10-20 kilometers.

However, we did suffer some casualties, and one in particular stands out. A technical sergeant from one of the rifle companies was hit by a shell fragment in the lower leg, between the knee and the ankle. It severed most of his lower leg. The bones had been crushed a few inches above his ankle, and most of the foot was hanging by the ligaments. When the fragment hit him, it must have been hot and seared the arteries and sealed them because he had not lost much blood. The wound was very painful, and any movement of his foot was agony.

He spoke up and pleaded, "Would you cut the foot off so I won't be in so much pain?" There were not any doctors with us at the time, so it was up to me to make the decision. I looked at his leg more carefully and came to the conclusion that the foot was so mangled that it never could be repaired. So I said, "I will after the morphine takes effect."

I gave him a shot of morphine and looked for the best instrument to cut off his foot. The only thing available was a straight razor that Sgt. Woods had picked up at a German army depot. I sterilized the razor and, with some trepidation, cut off his foot just above the ankle. The foot had just been hanging on by the flesh and perhaps tendons so the sharp razor cut through very easily. I cleaned up the stump, packed it with sulfanilamide powder and bound it up.

The sergeant was very relieved and seemed quite happy in spite of losing his foot. He started talking about the strange coincidences of the war. He said that the U.S. forces in the Pacific were now landing in the Philippines and, in civilian life, he had been a ship's pilot for the port of Manila. When he went into the service, his experience as a seaman had been disregarded, and he was placed into the Army and sent to Europe. His experience in the Philippines would have been valuable to the Navy in the Pacific.

Before we evacuated the sergeant, Cpl. Dazzo asked me what to do with the amputated foot. That question made me think a bit. Should I send it with the man? What do you do with an amputated foot? I did not believe the field hospitals could do anything with it because it was so smashed and badly mangled. I told Cpl. Dazzo to bury it.

It was too bad that our men were still being killed and maimed now that we were so near the end of the war in Europe. Everyone was becoming a little cautious to make sure they were not the last man to be killed or wounded. I now believed I would live through the war and finally get home.

May 6–8, 1945. Dolní Žandov (Dolzandov), Czechoslovakia

We left our position and joined the rest of the company, which had moved to Dolní Žandov. We were out in the country on a back road leading to Karlsbad, which was about 35 miles away. The countryside was wooded, and there were few houses on the road. There couldn't have been many people living near here because we saw quite a few deer in the woods as we drove to Dolní Žandov.

We set up the aid station in a tent because there were not any houses in the area. We knew hostilities were about over in Europe, and we probably would not have many more casualties. We had heard that the story about the Nazis' buildup and a last stand in the so-called Redoubt was a hoax. Except for our present action, the European war was over.

The division was advancing on the main road from Cheb to Karlsbad when, on May 7, 1945, we received the following notice to be read before the Retreat formation at 1715 hours on May 8, 1945:

> A representative of the German High Command signed the unconditional surrender of all German land, sea and air forces in Europe to the AEF and simultaneously to the Soviet High Command at 0141 hours Central European Time 7 May 45 under which all forces will cease active operations at 0001 hours 9 May 45.*

*Official notice from First Division headquaters; also in Danger Forward *(1947), page 394.*

Twenty-two

European War Over

May 9–22, 1945. Dolní Žandov (Dolzandov), Czechoslovakia

The day after the surrender, I heard the sound of many airplanes coming from the east. A little later, a huge air armada started coming toward us and passed directly overhead. I saw they were German war planes of all types. There were bombers, fighter planes and huge transport planes. They were flying low over our area. At first, I thought it might be some Germans who had refused to surrender and were either coming to attack or were going to that so-called Redoubt to fight longer. I soon found that the planes were full of German soldiers who did not want to surrender to the Russians and who did not want to be in the Russian occupation zone. They were flying well into the Allied zone and were surrendering to U.S forces. This was a welcome relief. The 1st Division was in the Russian occupation zone and, eventually, we would have to move back and turn this area over to the Russian army. That is why the Germans wanted to get much farther behind our positions.

The war was now over for most of us who had fought a long time in Europe and Africa. Some men in Europe might have to go to the Pacific but, if the point plan the Army had been talking about went into effect, some of us would get out of the service very soon. The aid station was now only set up for our own company sick call and for all practical purposes was shut down.

We had kept log books listing all the people who had gone through our aid station during the past three years of combat. This included the wounded, the dead, and the sick of all the different groups of people, such as U.S. soldiers (from many units besides the 1st Division), Germans, Italians, French, British, even Russians and civilians from all the countries we had been in during the past three years. I roughly totaled up the names, and it was a surprising number of over 20,000 people. The total number of days we were in actual combat in these three years was about 510, so we averaged about 39 people per day.

Our company, of 105 men, had the following number of battle casualties:

Killed in action	3
Wounded in action	48
Anxiety state (est.)	15
Total	66

The 1st Division had a complement of about 15,000 men. The 1st Division's total battle casualties were:

Killed in action	4,325
Missing in action	1,241
Wounded in action	15,457
Total	21,023

The division had participated in the following campaigns (the arrowhead denotes an assault landing):

Algeria–French Morocco ➡
Tunisia
Sicily ➡
Normandy ➡
Northern France
Rhineland
Ardennes-Alsace
Central Europe

Now that the hostilities had stopped, we could relax, take it easy and really clean up. Someone found an old bathtub somewhere (probably in a bombed-out building) and brought it back to the camp. We cleaned it out and started to take long soaking baths. We would have to heat up the water in big containers and pour it into the bathtub that was sitting in the field. We had plenty of time.

The division quartermaster discovered a large stock of German army supplies, so we were issued many things like kegs of beer, cases of wine and even cases of schnapps. Because of the proximity to Pilsen, we found the beer was very good. There was also a brewery nearby, and when I went to pick up some beer, I found that they kept the beer for aging purposes in large wooden tanks. Each contained about 2–3,000 gallons. One time I went there, I discovered that some men had not been able to open the valve so they had knocked the valve off, and the beer had all drained out. The cellar was filled with about three feet of beer. What a waste.

I mentioned before that everyone was collecting souvenirs. Now that we would be going home, everyone had to decide what souvenirs to take home, and the trading got quite intense. I traded my P-38 (Luger pistol) for a new 1000-power Lietz microscope. I had visions of going to medical school and figured it would come in handy.

Cleaning a liberated bathtub for the first bath in a year. *Left to right:* Pvt. Lynch and Sgt. McFarland.

Cleaned bathtub to go into use at Dolzandov. *Left to right:* Sgt. McFarland and Pvt. Lynch.

About the middle of May, the Army announced that some of us would be sent home under the point system. The number of points was based on length of service, time spent overseas, number of battles and number of medals received. This was all totaled up, and those with the largest numbers would be the first to leave. I had 128 points. This was a high number, so I was probably eligible to go home soon.

When the company commander told me that I was to leave with the first group, he also offered me a battlefield commission, and I could immediately become an officer. However, there was a condition attached. If I accepted a commission, I would have to sign up for several more years. I gave an immediate refusal. I told him I had had enough of war, and I wanted to resume a normal life.

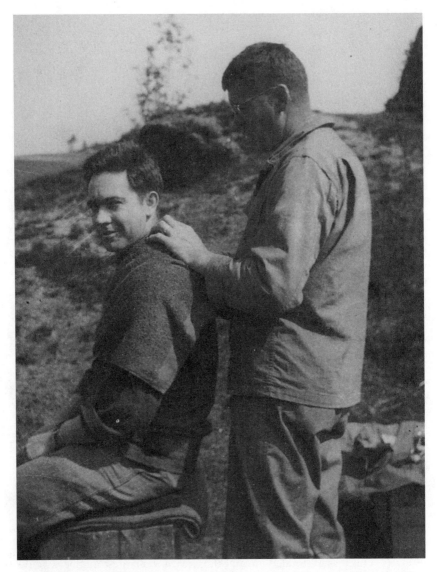

The war in Europe over, Sgt. Towne is getting a haircut from Pvt. Peter J. Gillen at Dolzandov, Czechoslovakia.

May 23, 1945. Dolzandov (Dolní Žandov), Czechoslovakia

This was the day I was to leave the company. I had been with many of these men for almost five years. I had mixed feelings about leaving them because I knew some of these men better than anyone else and perhaps I

Cpl. Brown is washing clothes in Dolzandov, Czechoslovakia.

would never feel so close to others again. Yet, I wanted to get out of the Army, and I intended to go back to college as soon as possible. While I realized that the war in the Pacific was not over and they might send the 1st Division to the Pacific for the invasion of Japan, I felt I had done enough, and others can take their chances in the rest of the war.

I left the company with Cpl. Randall, who also had a high number. We proceeded by truck to an assembly point at a former German army camp at a nearby railhead. This camp was a collection point for soldiers from many units who were to be sent back to the States. When there were enough men to fill a train and a train was available, we were to be transported to the port of Le Havre in France.

May 24–26, 1945. Former German army camp; Hof, Germany

We were able to visit a small town close by and go to a little German beer garden that had an outside patio and drink beer and listen to a small German band. It was pleasant. No one strayed far from the camp because no one wanted to miss this train.

The day before we left, we were all called to a formation, and the commanding officer of the camp spoke to us briefly and then awarded one of the men the Congressional Medal of Honor. He was a sergeant from another division and was an infantryman of Mexican-American extraction.

Washing clothes in Cormolain, Normandy. *Left to right:* **Sgt. Woods and Sgt. McFarland.**

May 27–31, 1945. Aboard troop train en route to port of Le Havre, France

    I boarded a freight car in a train made up of about 15–20 freight cars bound for Le Havre. There we would take a ship to the States. There were about 20–25 men to a freight car. These freight cars are much smaller than the ones in the United States. Each of us had a blanket so we could at least sit or lie down and talk, read or play cards and try to be comfortable.

It took us four days and nights to get to Le Havre. The reason for this long time was that the Allied air forces had crippled the European transportation system and destroyed many locomotives, rolling stock and bridges. Because we were going home, we did not have a high priority.

German railroad engineers were running the locomotives with help from our military police. We often would run out of coal and water, and sometimes the locomotives would break down. We frequently stopped for meals and sanitary stops but, basically, we used the freight cars as our home. Each morning, during one of our stops, we would get hot water from the locomotive to wash up. We still used our helmets as washbasins.

The rail beds were not very good and showed the effect of the Allied air force bombing. When we went over the temporary railroad bridge spanning the Rhine near Heidelberg, I looked out of both sides of the railroad car and could not see any part of the bridge under me. I could only see the water about 50–60 feet below. The bridge was so narrow that it seemed like we were floating in the air over the river. However, it was much safer crossing the Rhine this time than when I crossed the river at Remagen.

May 31–June 5, 1945. Le Havre, France

We finally made it to the camp near the French port. A big MP, who was in my boxcar, had been constantly complaining that his duffel bag was so heavy he could hardly lift it. When we arrived in Le Havre, he opened it to check his belongings and found that his buddy had placed a cannon ball in his bag while we were at the German camp, preparing to move. He had carried it from Czechoslovakia to Le Havre.

At Le Havre, we were at a large reception camp called "Lucky Strike." There were thousands of men here and about all we could do is eat and sleep. The lines for the meals were so long that one could stay in them all day just to get three meals. I usually settled for two meals.

The other man from my company, Cpl. Randall, had married a girl in England during our stay there over a year ago. He received permission to go back to England to join his wife before going back to the States. The rest of us just wanted to get back to the States as fast as possible. We were the first group from Europe to go back to the States, and I don't believe they knew exactly how to handle us. We stayed in tents (eight men to a tent) in this camp. Because we would have to carry our gear often before we got to our final destination, we started to discard heavy souvenirs.

We also had been told that we would be searched for weapons before we left because we could not bring any weapons back. As a result, the tents started to fill with many objects. In my tent, there were about five automatic weapons discarded. One was a German P-38, which was a type of German Luger. It was similar to the one I had traded to an infantryman for my new Lietz 1000-power microscope. I suspect that the troops running the Lucky Strike camp probably had the best selection of souvenirs in the E.T.O.

June 6–14, 1945. Aboard a Victory-class troop ship

I left France exactly one year after landing on D Day in 1944. The trip back to the States was uneventful and boring. We did have some rough weather, which made most of the men seasick. The motion of the Victory ship was not the violent pitching that causes many people to get seasick but rather a continual vibration that even gave me a slight headache. It did not really bother me, and I enjoyed myself at the mess hall. There were only a few soldiers most of the time, and the large mess hall was almost empty so there were no lines and plenty of food.

June 15, 1945. Fort Patrick Henry, Norfolk, Virginia

We finally docked at Norfolk, collected our gear and disembarked and stayed overnight in barracks. The next morning, we were split up according to destination. We all were to be sent back to the place we had been inducted, and so I was being sent to Fort Devens, Massachusetts.

We never had an inspection or went through any customs unit so we could have brought anything back. We all shouldered our gear and had a long hike to the trains. I had so much baggage and it was so heavy that I felt like discarding much it. My load consisted of all my issued gear plus the microscope (which was in a heavy wooden case), a new 16-mm Kodak movie camera and case (made in Germany), a small automatic pistol (I was bringing it back for a buddy to send to his wife), a camera and other souvenirs. I managed to get all my gear on board, and the train left for Fort Devens. It was a long, weary trip because we had to sit up the entire time and only stopped once, at Troy, New York for a change of locomotives.

June 16–23, 1945. Fort Devens, Massachusetts

When I arrived at Fort Devens, I was told that I would be processed in a few days and could go on pass. I called my parents, and they picked me up. They lived within 40 miles of Fort Devens. I saw them for the first time in over three years.

It was strange to be in a house. It was even stranger to go out and try to visit old friends. They were all in the service, and none of my old friends were around, except one who was recovering from wounds.

When I returned to Fort Devens to get discharged, I found Sgt. Woods was there, and he had just been discharged. He had left the company several weeks after me and had flown back in an Army air force transport plane. He had arrived at Devens before me.

I was discharged from the Army the next day, on June 23, 1945. During the discharge process, I was given a Bronze Star medal, my back pay and a ruptured duck lapel pin. This was exactly one month after I left the company in Europe. I had been in the Army for four years and eight months. During that time, I had had only two ten-day furloughs, so I decided to take the summer off.

Because I planned to go back to school, I had to immediately enroll in a school. I first went to Harvard University to see if I could get into its medical school program. I was given a hard time at Harvard because they said I would have to start all over. They said I had been out of school too long, and none of my past credits would count. I could not see starting all over, so I went back to Northeastern University in Boston, where I had been before the war. They accepted all my past credits, and I immediately enrolled for the fall term.

I found that Sgt. Woods and Sgt. Sherman, who had been in our company, were planning to go to school in Boston. We decided to room together when school started in the fall. I was to find a place in Boston for all of us to live.

Twenty-three

Reflections

It has been nearly sixty years since I entered the Army on October 16, 1940. This was a long time ago and, yet, some of the memories are as vivid as if it was a few weeks ago. I suppose you never forget the times you are really scared and were wondering if you would live to see the next day.

As the war progressed, and I saw more of the death and destruction brought on by the war, I was glad I was in the medical corps because in this mad world of war at least I was doing something constructive. I was helping to save the lives of not only our own men but anyone who was sick and wounded, including the enemy and civilians.

You never forget the horror of seeing men lying dead and wounded all around you and thinking that it could be me and it may be me unless I do something quick. Yet, often there was nothing that could be done except to continue to do your job and try to forget about the danger. You must keep busy or you can lose control of yourself.

Most soldiers are somewhat mentally prepared to see dead and wounded men. However, I think that combat fatigue, which occurred frequently, is one of the most frightening experiences to soldiers when they first see it happen to men they know. We had many men come through our aid station with anxiety state, combat fatigue or whatever you might call it. To me, they were real battle casualties. While it seems that most of the combat fatigue occurs in men new to battle action, it also occurs in men who have had much combat time. Perhaps, the strain is cumulative and they break under the continued strain. I often wondered if the new men broke down because they had not had enough training, or if it was inherent in their makeup and would have occurred in civilian life if they had encountered any severe problem. I also wondered if the men we sent back recovered. We never heard from any of the men while we were in the service, and it wasn't until years later that I found out that some men in my company had totally recovered.

In some respects, our division was fortunate because it had trained together as a unit for several years before the first combat, and we had relatively few incidents of combat fatigue until we started to get replacements. When the replacements came in at a time of tough combat, the incidence of combat fatigue among the replacements would be high. I often wondered if one problem in the Vietnam War was that the men would go to Vietnam for one year and then would go home. Then, you might not have the mixture of veterans and new men that is considered ideal for a fighting unit.

Our division was a good mixture for an assault unit in that most of the men were between 20 and 30 years old and had over two years in the same organization. Thus, it was a combination of battle-hardened veterans and new replacements. Because this was a regular Army division, it had many West Point–trained officers. Many think this mix of dedicated officers and enlisted men make an ideal combat unit. The division also had an extremely high esprit de corps, and the men believed that there was no unit better in any army.

When I left the Army, I was overjoyed. I could now start my life again. I no longer had to wonder *Will I ever get out of this? Will I live through this war?* It did not take long to feel that something was missing and, for a while, I could not figure out what it was. It was not until I had many interactions with other people that I understood what it was. All people had a front, a reserve, a poise that was not true, or to me, not honest. It was very difficult, if not impossible, to attain the feeling of a bond or perhaps true friendship with others.

Why was this? Was it because everyone had changed, or had I changed? After giving it some thought, I came to the conclusion that I was the one who had changed. I started to think about when this change might have occurred. I knew that when I first entered the Army and for the first year there was not much of a change in how I felt toward others. Our company had the standard mixture of people, and the saying in the Army was that, if you wanted to become an NCO you should get into trouble and make a lot of noise so you would be noticed and, eventually, you would become an NCO when an opening was available. This was true in the peacetime Army.

It started to change after we went to England and was very evident after our first taste of combat. When we went into action, some of the people who were promoted could not or would not perform. There was a gradual reshuffle of people, and many less-vocal people started to assume the positions of leadership. A more competent, less blustery company emerged. There was little facade in the men, and everyone knew where they stood. Thus, it was not until I was in the Army and in combat that I really felt a true bond with others. It was in this environment that you come to depend on each other no matter what the situation. You would not hesitate to do whatever was needed to help the other. This would be expected whatever the cost and that includes the ultimate cost of your own life. Not only would you expect others to do the same, you would be certain of it.

When I got out of the service, I found that this was the big failing in civilian life and that, in the context of this definition of friendship, you do not have many true friends. The only relationship that is similar, is the one with my wife and, hopefully, with my children. Perhaps this is why many people think that soldiers have a good time in war, because they have some very good recollections. I believe the reason is that they saw the best in relationships with other people. This is difficult, if not impossible, to duplicate in civilian life, or in the peacetime Army, or even in the service in wartime unless you experience long, difficult battles.

It is not until the esprit de corps of a unit builds up that you get what is called the pride of a unit which makes some fighting groups much better than others. This, plus the fear of being a coward, is stronger than the fear of death. It also cuts down on casualties. I believe this type of relationship exists in other tightly knit organizations, such as terrorist groups.

This did not seem to occur very much with the troops fighting in the Vietnam war. This is why I think the Vietnam War was so different from other wars. People were there for only a year, and there was a continual rotation of men in a unit. After the original men were rotated, the continuity would be broken, and the elan, spirit, camaraderie or whatever you call it was diminished and perhaps lost entirely.

In combat conditions, you find that time becomes meaningless. Although the unit moves from place to place, there is a dreadful monotony. After the period of combat is over, everything runs together, and it is hard to remember when something happened. It is only when some life-threatening situation involves you that the time would be vivid. That is why the daily log of events, as brief as the notes were, became so useful in putting the incidents in the proper chronological order.

It also can be years later before you find out what really was going on during some periods of confusing action. For example, when our group landed at Normandy, we thought we had been left at the east end of Omaha beach. We actually had been set ashore at Fox Green, where the German gunners on the cliffs looked almost directly down on the beach. This was where E Company of the 16th Infantry and E Company of the 116 Infantry were put ashore in error (by the Navy). Both units were cut to pieces by the Germans. When we landed later, their bodies were still there, and that part of the beach was still in German hands. We did not realize how lucky we were that we got out alive.

War is very wasteful. It seems that many of the best people get killed and maimed. The reason for this is that natural selection, driven by the horrors of combat, forces the best men to take over and, of course, they are most likely to be casualties.

Warfare is a paradox. It is futile, useless, horrible and, yet, it can bring out the best qualities in people. It is too bad that the élan of war cannot be transferred to civilian life. So much good could be accomplished.

Index